THE COMERAGH, GALTEE, KNOCKMEALDOWN AND SLIEVE BLOOM MOUNTAINS
A WALKING GUIDE

JOHN G. O'DWYER is a travel consultant, a regular contributor to *The Irish Times* and the author of *Pilgrim Paths in Ireland: A Guide*. A keen hillwalker and rock climber, he founded the Mid-Tipp Hillwalkers Club and has almost thirty years' experience of leading hillwalking and mountain-climbing groups in Ireland, the UK, Europe and Africa.

www.pilgrimpath.ie

Disclaimer

Hillwalking and mountaineering are risk sports. The author and the publisher accept no responsibility for any injury, loss or inconvenience sustained by anyone using this guidebook.

Advice to Readers

Every effort is made by our authors to ensure the accuracy of our guidebooks. However, changes can occur after a book has been printed, including changes to rights of way. If you notice discrepancies between this guidebook and the facts on the ground, please let us know, either by email to enquiries@collinspress.ie or by post to The Collins Press, West Link Park, Doughcloyne, Wilton, Cork, T12 N5EF, Ireland.

THE COMERAGH, GALTEE, KNOCKMEALDOWN AND SLIEVE BLOOM MOUNTAINS
A WALKING GUIDE

JOHN G. O'DWYER

The Collins Press

Published in 2018 by
The Collins Press
West Link Park
Doughcloyne
Wilton
Cork
T12 N5EF
Ireland

First published in 2012 as *Tipperary & Waterford: A Walking Guide*

© John G. O'Dwyer 2012, 2018, 2021, 2022

Photographs © John G. O'Dwyer unless otherwise credited

John G. O'Dwyer has asserted his moral right to be identified as the author of this work in accordance with the Copyright and Related Rights Act 2000. All photographs courtesy of the author unless otherwise credited.

All rights reserved. The material in this publication is protected by copyright law. Except as may be permitted by law, no part of the material may be reproduced (including by storage in a retrieval system) or transmitted in any form or by any means, adapted, rented or lent without the written permission of the copyright owners. Applications for permissions should be addressed to the publisher.

A CIP record for this book is available from the British Library.

Paperback ISBN: 978-1-84889-347-4

Design and typesetting by Fairways Design
Typeset in Myriad Pro
Printed in Białostockie Zakłady Graficzne SA

Photographs
Page 1: Approaching Laghtea summit, County Tipperary;
pages 2–3: The view south from the Devilsbit, County Tipperary.

Contents

Quick-reference route summary	6
Introduction	9
Using this book	14

The Slieve Bloom Mountains — 16
Walk 1: Glenbarrow and the Ridge of Capard — 18
Walk 2: The Central Slieve Bloom — 23
Walk 3: Arderin — 28
Walk 4: The Eastern Slieve Bloom — 33
Walk 5: Giant's Grave and the Spink — 37

The Slievefelim Hills — 41
Walk 6: The Eamonn a Chnoic Loop — 42
Walk 7: Keeper Hill (Slievekimalta) — 46
Walk 8: The Knockalough Loop — 51

The Comeragh Mountains — 56
Walk 9: The Nire Valley Coums — 57
Walk 10: The Mahon Falls and Coumtay — 62
Walk 11: Coumshingaun and Crotty's Lough — 67
Walk 12: The Circuit of Glenary — 72
Walk 13: Knockanaffrin Ridge — 77
Walk 14: Coum Iarthar — 81

The Galtee Mountains — 86
Walk 15: The Circuit of Glencushnabinna — 87
Walk 16: Lyracappul and Temple Hill — 92
Walk 17: Lough Muskry and Greenane — 97
Walk 18: Galtymore from the Black Road — 101

The Knockmealdown Mountains — 107
Walk 19: Mount Melleray Abbey and the Knockmealdown Ridge — 108
Walk 20: Bay Lough, the Sugarloaf and Knockmoylan — 113
Walk 21: The High Knockmealdowns — 118
Walk 22: The Western Knockmealdowns from Crow Hill Car Park — 123

The Arra Mountains — 127
Walk 23: The Millennium Cross and Tountinna — 128

Other County Tipperary Walks — 133
Walk 24: Knockanroe and Silvermines Ridge — 134
Walk 25: Slievenamon and Killusty Cross — 139
Walk 26: Aherlow, Slievenamuck and the Jubilee 2000 Memorial — 144
Walk 27: The Grange Crag Loop — 149
Walk 28: Devilsbit Mountain — 154

Quick-Reference Route Table

Location	No.	Walk name
Slieve Blooms	1	Glenbarrow and the Ridge of Capard
	2	The Central Slieve Bloom
	3	Arderin
	4	The Eastern Slieve Bloom
	5	Giant's Grave and the Spink
Slievefelim Hills	6	Eamonn a Chnoic Loop
	7	Keeper Hill (Slievekimalta)
	8	The Knockalough Loop
Comeraghs	9	The Nire Valley Coums
	10	The Mahon Falls and Coumtay
	11	Coumshingaun and Crotty's Lough
	12	The Circuit of Glenary
		Option 2
	13	Knockanaffrin Ridge
	14	Coum Iarthar
Galtees	15	The Circuit of Glencushnabinna
	16	Lyracappul and Temple Hill
	17	Lough Muskry and Greenane
	18	Galtymore from the Black Road
		Option 2: from King's Yard
Knockmealdowns	19	Mount Melleray Abbey and the Knockmealdown Ridge
	20	Bay Lough, the Sugarloaf and Knockmoylan
		Option 2
	21	The High Knockmealdowns
	22	The Western Knockmealdowns from Crow Hill Car Park
Arra Mountains	23	The Millennium Cross and Tountinna
County Tipperary (Other)	24	Knockanroe and Silvermines Ridge
	25	Slievenamon and Killusty Cross
	26	Aherlow, Slievenamuck and the Jubilee 2000 Memorial
	27	The Grange Crag Loop
	28	Devilsbit Mountain
		Longer option

County	Grade	Time	Ascent	Distance	Page
Laois	2	3 hours	180m	10km	18
Laois/Offaly	2/3	4½ hours	195m	15km	23
Laois/Offaly	2/3	45 minutes	80m	1.5km	28
Laois	2/3	5 hours	355m	20km	33
Laois/Offaly	2	4 hours	240m	14km	37
Tipperary	2	2½ hours	150m	8km	42
Tipperary	2/3	3½ hours	550m	14km	46
Tipperary	2/3	3 hours	320m	10km	51
Waterford	4	5 hours	790m	15km	57
Waterford	4	3½ hours	390m	6.5km	62
Waterford	4	5 hours	730m	12km	67
Waterford	3	3 hours	240m	11km	72
Waterford	3	4½ hours	470m	13.5km	72
Waterford	4	4 hours	500m	11.5km	77
Waterford	4	4½ hours	570m	8km	81
Tipperary/Limerick	4	5 hours	1,025m	12.5km	87
Limerick	4	5 hours	765m	12km	92
Tipperary	4	4½ hours	635m	12.5km	97
Tipperary/Limerick	4	3½ hours	610m	9km	101
Tipperary/Limerick	4	4 hours	700m	10km	106
Waterford	4	4½ hours	580m	11.5km	108
Tipperary/Waterford	3/4	3 hours	480m	7km	113
Tipperary/Waterford	4	4½ hours	860m	11km	113
Tipperary/Waterford	4	6½ hours	1,215m	20km	118
Tipperary/Waterford	3	4 hours	360m	9km	123
Tipperary	3	5 hours	350m	16km	128
Tipperary	3	3 hours	255m	7km	134
Tipperary	3	4½ hours	530m	13km	139
Tipperary	2	3½ hours	170m	13km	144
Tipperary	1	2 hours	160m	6km	149
Tipperary	2	1½ hours	240m	5km	154
Tipperary	3	3 hours	310m	9km	158

Walkers on the moraines above Lough Muskry.

Introduction

No matter how much we idealise them, mountains are just inanimate uplifts of soil and rock. Nevertheless, there is something about these great edifices that inescapably draws our eyes, for they are nature's foremost attention-grabbers. Far more influential even than the sum of their parts, soaring peaks immediately define the lands below, while exerting a magnetic attraction to, and sense of wonder about, the highest places. With summits that were entirely unknown to people in the surrounding valleys, it is almost inevitable that the world's highest mountain would be saddled with strange tales of malevolent demons and angry deities. The forbidding tops of the world's great mountains, such as Kilimanjaro, Mont Blanc and Everest, have, therefore, evoked equal measures of fear and reverence among upward-gazing people, with early climbers commonly regarded as reckless tempters of fate.

But size is only part of the story when it comes to mountains and this is particularly the case with the uplands of the Irish midlands and south. There is no mountaintop here that cannot be reached by a reasonably fit walker, doing nothing more technical than putting one foot in front of the other, which means these modest ranges have been accessible to humans since the dawn of history. Small wonder then, that the summits here did not become distant objects of reverence and fear. Instead, they became a unifying feature of the landscape and were purposefully woven into the myths and legends used to bind communities since pre-Christian times.

Like ageing divas, however, mountains appear to show their best side to the uninitiated when appreciated from afar. Romantic tales are most alluring when the diva or hill is far away – on stage or horizon. Get closer and the magic may at first be lessened.

Most of the mountains of the midlands and south consist of rounded peaks or undulating plateaus that are cold, windy and eroded, while very often mist obscures the wished-for view. Those who come to these highlands with a vision informed by the idealised canvases of outstanding painters like Paul Henry are almost certainly bound for disappointment. And it isn't just the weather or the terrain that may spoil the romance, it is also the work of man.

Human influence is everywhere. There are trig points, sculptures, deflector masts, tombs, crosses, altars, towers, huts, shelters and, of course, the ubiquitous cairns. The historic, the aesthetic, the commercial and the spiritual all jostle for the psychological dominance offered by the highest place.

But this should not be off-putting, for wilderness – when defined as landscape unaltered by human intervention – exists nowhere on this island and those who seek it are likely to remain unfulfilled. Every Irish landscape – from brook to beach, mountain to marsh, hedge to heath – is shaped by human intervention.

Just as a seascape is enhanced by a scrap of sail and a meadow by gambolling horseflesh, the upland experience is at its most rewarding when we come to understand how high places have contributed to human endeavour by seeking out and understanding the clues in the landscape. A booley in a high place tells a tale of contribution to human survival; a working farmstead on a mountainside demonstrates the success of this contribution; a ruined cottage confirms a battle lost. Politically, economically or spiritually – depending on perceived need – the powerful symbolism and economic value of our mountains have been exploited historically to sustain and bind communities.

No matter where you wander, you will find the highlands of Offaly, Tipperary, Laois and Waterford are loaded with history and legend. The secret is to do a little research before you ascend. Then press the pause button on your frenetic 21st-century life while you head out among these much-weathered hills and see the landscape spring to life as a lavishly illustrated storybook. Most likely you will return enriched by your upland experience and looking forward to your next hill-country outing – for once established, a hillwalking routine is a gift that keeps on giving.

Safety on the hills

This spirit of adventure lurks somewhere within us all. It is this pursuit of challenge and uncertainty that drives us forward to seek higher planes of endeavour and to push back the frontiers of the possible. It finds expression in the successes of Amundsen and Hillary, in the failures of Mallory and Scott – and within every hillwalker who struggles bravely to reach a modest Irish hilltop.

All very worthwhile and challenging, of course, assuming that, unlike Mallory and Scott, everyone comes back in one piece. While it is statistically true that the most dangerous part of any climb is the road journey to the trailhead, it should, nevertheless, be kept in mind that accidents do happen in the hill country, and they mostly occur when and where we least expect them.

Hillwalkers come to grief more often on easy slopes or very commonly in that moment of relaxation at the end of a hard climb. The descent is also a prime time when climbers snatch defeat from victory, since this is when we are generally more tired, less watchful and subconsciously feel the day's work is done. Nonetheless, those whose first experience of our high country comes on a cloudless, benign day will wonder how we can possibly have so many mountain accidents, and even fatalities.

The answer is, of course, that while in Spain the rain may indeed fall mainly on the plain, in Ireland it falls predominantly on the uplands with the result that there are many days of low cloud, breath-robbing gales and louring drizzle. Without direct experience, it's hard to imagine how – since Irish mountains aren't very high – the weather on the peaks can be so different from that at sea level. It is all too easy to get caught out, unprepared for the conditions, and the consequences can range from uncomfortable to desperately serious. The forecast for Cahir may be for a 20km/h breeze and temperature of 10 ºC: on Galtymore summit this could mean -5 ºC and gusts of 70km/h.

Distant views of mountains speak tantalisingly of freedom and adventure, but seldom hint towards the hardships and dangers that can await. So, if we want to wander safely among even the most modest Irish mountains we must understand that these are places where natural forces still prevail and will give no quarter to our puny endeavours. We must expect rain as often as sunshine, storms as well as gentle breezes and all-obscuring drizzle as frequently as magical moments.

The first rule when heading into the hills is to think optimistically but pack pessimistically. There is a need for full body cover and when heading up onto the higher summits we should have a waterproof jacket, a fleece, over-trousers, two pairs of gloves and a balaclava. Not only is it more pleasant to be warm and dry, it is also a lot safer since we function better when we are comfortable.

The second rule is to carry food and a warm drink since hillwalking is a strenuous activity. It is also prudent to bring along some emergency rations in case you get delayed or benighted. For this purpose, carbohydrates are best as they are easiest for your body to convert quickly into energy. Also, carry a mobile phone as a backup but do not rely on it totally – Murphy's Law suggests it won't work at the time you most need it.

The third rule is being aware that having a map, compass and GPS in your rucksack is about as useful for route finding as a desert lighthouse unless you know how to use them. You must learn to route-find competently in mist if you intend having recourse to the high summits. Otherwise, stick with walks that offer a navigational handrail. These can be the clifftops above a coum as at Coumshingaun, a continuous fence similar to the many that exist in the west Knockmealdowns, or a well-defined mountain track such as that leading to Lough Muskry in the Galtee Mountains.

Finally, it is important to remember the hills should foster our spirit of self-reliance, so here are some basic questions you should be able to answer before setting out, if you want to make certain you are the person taking off your walking boots at the end of the day:

- Do you know where you are going and have you the navigational skills to get there and back in poor visibility?
- Have you estimated how long the walk will take?
- Are you sure it is within your ability and that of your companions to complete it safely with time to spare before nightfall?
- Finally, does someone know your intended route and estimated time of return?
- Is your mobile phone fully powered?

If the answer is 'yes' to these questions, you are now set for memorable days in the mountains of the Irish midlands and south.

Facing page: the western cliffs of Coum Iarthar, County Waterford.

Using This Book

Walking Times

Walking times in this book were calculated by hiking each route at a consistent but not particularly hurried pace and then recording only the time spent actually on the move. Obviously, times will vary considerably with individual fitness and chosen pace, so the walking times quoted here should be treated as broad approximations only, with completion times often rising considerably in poor conditions.

Walk Grades

Walks are graded 1 to 4 based on level of difficulty, with 1 being the easiest and 4 the most challenging. None of the routes involves any technical climbing skills, but under snow and ice conditions all grade 4 routes and some lower grades become serious ventures, possibility requiring use of a full suite of winter mountaineering skills.

Grade 1: Suited for beginners or families with children, these trails are at low-level and follow well-constructed paths offering firm underfoot conditions. There are no navigational difficulties as the routes are well signposted throughout and involve nothing in the way of serious ascent.

Grade 2: Suited for those with some experience of walking in wilder spaces, these walks generally follow waymarked paths with good underfoot conditions, but may involve some short, but taxing, ascents. Trails may cross upland landscapes with some sections of open moorland and rough ground requiring navigational awareness.

Grade 3: Routes traverse informal paths, often with demanding underfoot conditions, and also trackless mountainside. Walks can lead to high altitude and involve coping with relatively steep terrain. Generally not waymarked, these routes require robust navigational skills in what can sometimes be featureless terrain.

Grade 4: Paths are generally informal or non-existent and underfoot conditions can be quite demanding. There may be prolonged sections of rocky and unstable ground. A full array of navigation skills may be required in poor weather. The ability to deal with hazards such as cliffs edges, high winds, scree and steep ground will commonly be required. Basic scrambling skills, such as required on the circuit of Coumshingaun, will come into play occasionally.

View north over clear-felled forestry in Walk 5: Giant's Grave and the Spink.

The Slieve Bloom Mountains

An economist is reputed to have remarked, 'I know this works well in practice, but will it work in theory?' He might have been referring to rambling the Slieve Blooms, an activity that, from a purely theoretical perspective, appears to offer little for discerning hikers. There is the absence of majestic summits, the often-unsympathetic terrain, along with the difficulty of uncovering circular walks; all this has moved conventional wisdom regularly to decry these uplands. Indeed, for those whose sole quest is the instant gratification of 'wow moments' in the uplands, the Slieve Blooms are probably not the ticket, for, like Brussels sprouts and coffee, these flattened hills are an acquired taste.

The limestone overlay that once soared to Alpine heights has been worn down to the underlying sandstone, which has flattened the mountaintops and thus provided the ideal waterlogged conditions for the creation of Ireland's most extensive blanket bog. With this greatly reduced stature, the Blooms have sometimes been unkindly likened to a huge tube of used toothpaste. This moniker may not be totally unfair for it is undeniable that Ireland's most centrally situated uplands lack the great coums and five-star ridges offered by the younger mountains of Ireland's south-west.

Whatever conventional theory might say, however, you can be assured that for those who plan their outing, the Blooms do work well, often exceeding expectations for even the most perceptive walkers. At almost 400 million years, they lay claim to being among Europe's oldest ranges, while also carrying a majestic appellation evoking – often very real – images of flower-fragrant hillsides. Reminiscent of England's Peak District, which, puzzlingly for many, contains no mountain peaks, the Blooms are not memorable for their spear-point summits; indeed, most look as if they have had a once-over from a giant sander. Instead, genuine pleasure comes with the many sequestered glens that once supported vibrant communities and still hold many subtle monuments to past endeavour. Stick to the trails and you will enjoy a very real sensation of being detached from modernity amid a captivating uplift from Ireland's central plain that comes alive on mostly gentle outings, making the Blooms eminently suitable for ramblers wishing for time to stand and stare.

WALK 1:
Glenbarrow and the Ridge of Capard

Grade:	2
Time:	3 hours
Ascent:	180m
Distance:	10 km
Map:	OSi *Discovery* Series sheet 54

Start & Finish: Rosenallis village, County Laois, is 6km from Mountmellick on the R422. From here, follow the minor road at the Catholic church. After 2.5km, swing right and continue for 2km more before turning left at a crossroads, signposted Glenbarrow. The car park at the end of this road is your starting point.

Suitability: The route is entirely on waymarked tracks and presents few navigational difficulties. The terrain can be uneven, however, and includes several boggy patches, so boots are required.

Glenbarrow is undoubtedly the queen of the Slieve Bloom Glens. It is by far the most frequented location in these mountains and even a cursory visit reveals why. Examples of almost all that is subtly wondrous about these uplands has been shoehorned into this heavily glaciated little valley, which is a place not so much to be walked as explored.

To become acquainted with this cornucopia of wonder, start from the sylvan car park at Glenbarrow, **N367 082**. Follow the red directional arrows downhill, along an enclosed lane, to what was once a ford in the nascent River Barrow. Continue by swinging left along an atmospheric woodland path, with your footsteps muffled pleasantly by carpets of fallen pine needles and also by the soothing sound of rushing water. Across the river, the remarkably steep banks were created when great glaciers that surmounted the north side of the Blooms melted during the last ice age, leaving behind this huge glacial moraine. The steepness of the terrain made commercial forestation impractical and so this area has reverted delightfully to natural woodland.

Walk 1: Glenbarrow and the Ridge of Capard

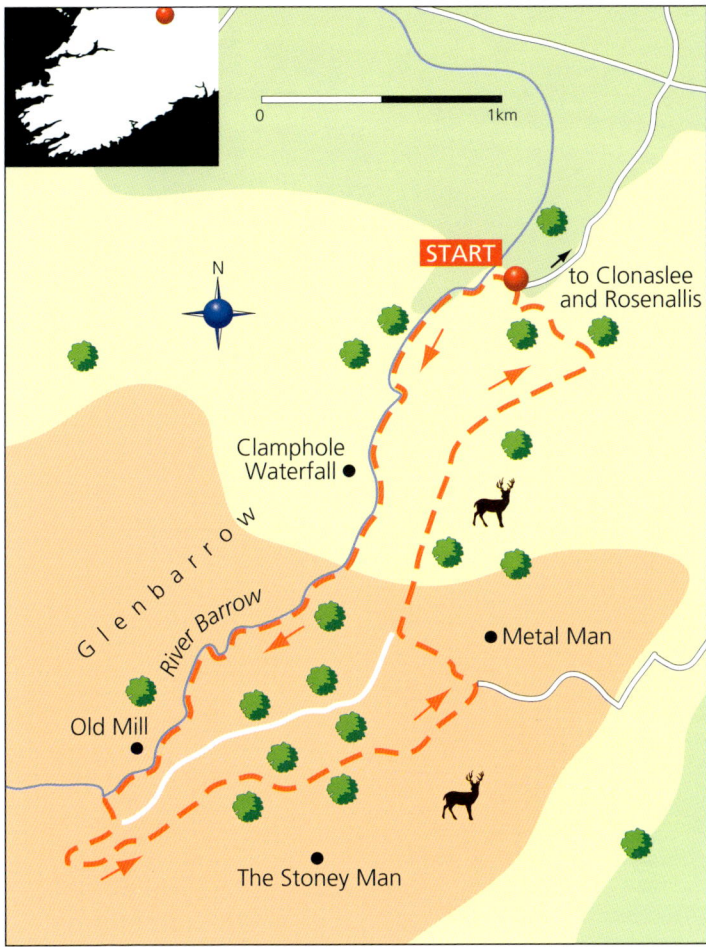

Soon, you will pass a hut and then an open area by the river where the underlying sandstone has been exposed. This rock type makes an excellent building material and is the floor of a nineteenth-century quarry from which pavement was extracted.

Upriver now, where next to capture your attention will be the three-drop Clamphole Waterfall. Here is a favourite haunt of families in summer and a spectacular place after heavy rain, when an angry torrent cascades down. At any time, it is a good place to pause and gaze awhile at the mesmerically soothing waters. Here, they appear in a great hurry to morph into Ireland's second longest river, coalesce with the Suir and Nore, before making a grand entrance to the Atlantic Ocean at Waterford Harbour.

The multi-drop Clamphole Waterfall.

You may also reflect that Clamphole is a good example of how waterfalls continually move backwards as the underlying rock is eroded by the plunge pool beneath the falls. This eventually causes the harder overlying rock to collapse under its own weight, thus moving the falls upstream.

Now the path roughens a bit as it leads nonchalantly above a deep gorge, which the river has carved into the mountainside, before continuing to a parting with the arrows of the Waterfall Loop. If time is short you can follow the blue arrow (left) and steeply uphill, then go left again on a forest road from where a straight ahead at every junction will convey you directly back to Glenbarrow car park. This option is shorter by 6km, 80m of ascent and 1¾ hours. The more rewarding option, however, is to descend and regain the banks of the infant Barrow. The Slieve Bloom Way proceeds over a sturdy footbridge here, but you continue by following the riverbank to gain an area of cleared forest where exist the ruins of a surprisingly sturdy stone farmhouse. Soon after are the remnants of a watermill, which was operated by the local Gallagher family and used for grinding oats mostly – the corn crop better suited to the wetter, cooler upland environment that once rivalled the potato as a food source. The strangely poignant

Walk 1: Glenbarrow and the Ridge of Capard

The Ridge of Capard car park.

remains of the grinding stone are still visible beside the stream and act as a reminder that this area once supported an industrious community, which in Glenbarrow's present heavily forested state is difficult to imagine. It is important to remember, however, that it was only after local families abandoned the valley that the Forestry Commission purchased the lands and a programme of intense afforestation commenced in the 1960s.

Beyond the mill site, it is uphill on a narrow gravel path to gain a forestry road. Then it is right and, soon after, left and uphill to a gateway, which takes you above the claustrophobic confines of the valley and onto the refreshingly airy expanse of Capard Ridge. Soon the red arrows point right and along a boardwalk that will eventually deposit you at an elevated viewing point offering extensive panoramas.

Here, you will observe that the Ridge of Capard consists of an elongated heathery crest, consisting of the relatively flat and thus poorly drained upland terrain that leads to the formation of a blanket bog. Capard is bookended at one extremity by the 2.5m cairn known as the Stoney Man and at the other by a pair of huge communication masts, that have been dubbed the Metal Man (as opposed to the more appropriate Metal Men). Further afield, there are splendid vistas on offer over Ireland's richly embroidered central plain with all four provinces in view at once. The Dublin, Wicklow and Blackstairs Mountains act as a suitably dramatic backdrop to the eastwards outlook; to the north the panorama encompasses almost all the Irish midlands before misting to the Cuilcagh Mountains on the Fermanagh/Cavan border while, to the south, a great prospect stretches away to the distant Galtee Mountains.

Arrows now point along the boardwalk to the Ridge of Capard car park and then down a stony lane to a right turn onto a forestry road. Veering right at a three-way junction, it is onwards until the arrows point to a boardwalk leading downhill to a forestry road, which emerges beside a barrier. Here, it is just a short ramble right to your start point where you will likely conclude that Glenbarrow is hard to beat for a genuine away-from-it-all experience that is achieved as a reward for modest effort.

Returning to Glenbarrow.

WALK 2:
The Central Slieve Bloom

Grade:	2/3
Time:	4½ hours
Ascent:	195m
Distance:	15km
Map:	OSi, *Discovery* Series sheet 54

Start & Finish: From Mountrath, County Laois, follow the signs for the Slieve Bloom Mountains and Kinnitty. Park at the sign for Gorteenameale Eco Walk.

Suitability: A reasonably unchallenging circuit offering mostly walker-friendly terrain but also including some tedious moorland, so wear boots. This route also traverses open mountaintop where disorientation is a possibility in mist, so prepare for this eventuality.

Considering the expansive area covered and the central position they occupy in the Irish landscape, surprisingly little has been written about the Slieve Blooms. One book that was dedicated, however, to getting beneath the obvious in the Blooms unearthed a treasure trove of wonder in mountains where people have lived and farmed for many generations. Describing each walk as 'a string of pearls', Tom Joyce, in his exquisitely illustrated little book *Bladhma – Walks of Discovery in the Slieve Blooms*, uncovered a legacy of historic artefacts, mythological resonances and natural wonders awaiting the culturally curious rambler.

To go in search of your own 'string of pearls', a good place to start is by heading west from Gorteenameale ('Garden of the summits', **N280 025**) along a woodland path. When the main path goes left, continue straight ahead, enjoying expansive views south across the fertile Laois countryside. When the trail peters out, your route lies west past a large cairn on an informal track that follows a forestry firebreak. This track eventually crosses a small ravine at a marker post, before rising to gain a forest. Don't enter the forest but instead swing right along the forest edge before tagging

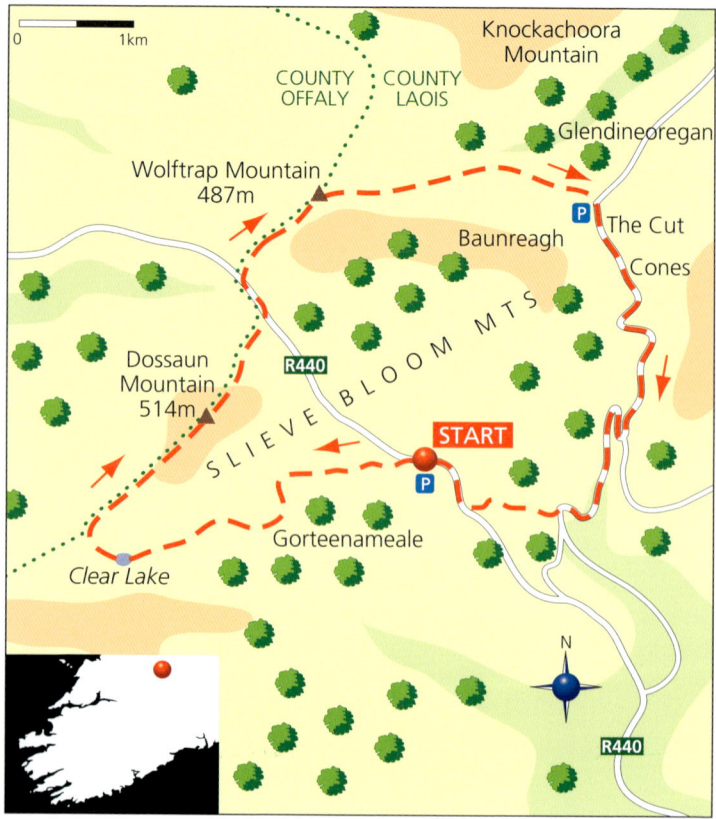

the track through the trees to gain open mountainside. The casual path passes by a single marker as grand views unfold west over Carroll's Hill and Arderin. Soon after, the first objective for today's walk will make its appearance, although you will almost be upon it before you see it. Clear Lake is quite tiny, about the size of a large pond but is remarkable for the freshness of its waters, located as they are in the midst of blanket bog and also for the almost perfect symmetry of its circular shoreline. You could imagine a meteorite had dropped from the sky to create this perfect ring of unreflecting water.

From here, convenient waymarkers will provide you with a handrail north across a great vastness of wind-tortured moorlands where time appears to have stood still. Indeed, the area may evoke images of Yorkshire and *Wuthering Heights*, and have you pondering that here is the perfect location for a re-enactment of the Brontë classic. In summer, watch out for the hen harrier, a large winged bird of prey that may rise suddenly in

Frosty morning above Glendineoregan.

acrobatic flight. An inhabitant of high moorlands, it has been declining in numbers in recent years due to changes in land use and has now been provided with a sanctuary in the upland bogs of the Blooms.

Gaining a low bank marking the Offaly/Laois border, go right and follow it to the lonesome but undistinguished top of Dossaun Mountain (514m) and then onwards through expansive heathlands until the bank finally deposits you on the R440. This road was built in the eighteenth century as a turnpike linking Mountrath to Kilcormac, with a toll payable by all who used the route.

At this point you have the option of simply going right and following the road directly back to Gorteenameale after a pleasant twenty-minute stroll. The more adventurous option takes you left, into County Offaly, and after a short distance, to the severely rutted track leading right from the R440 that serves the giant communication masts now colonising the highest elevation of Wolftrap Mountain: an unforgettable appellation that may have you evoking visions of a not-so-distant era, when wolves roamed the Irish landscape, but the reality is less dramatic. The trig pillar stands trackside and so Wolftrap can be for day trippers with good auto suspensions, a drive-in mountaintop.

From the trig point, continue across the plateau of Cones, which is overlaid with deep and uneven blanket bog. This section is mercifully short, however, and your reward for effort is an expansive view north over

The Slieve Bloom Way at Baunreagh.

the central plain until after about a kilometre, when you should pick up a forest track leading to the car park above the head of Glendineoregan. Here, the way is south through the defile of The Cut, which in the eighteenth century was hewn laboriously through the unforgivingly hard sandstone by human hand, with two of the workers leaving their initials carved for posterity.

About 2.5km on, a sign points right and downhill for Baunreagh. Now, heavily forested with pine and spruce, this valley once supported a thriving community. Joyce recounts that here was the scene of a nineteenth-century experiment on rendering mountain land productive, which was conducted by one William Stuart Trench. The reclamation project worked so well that it employed over 200 labourers and successfully produced potatoes and even corn. According to Joyce, the 'efforts at reclamation in Baunreagh came to the attention of many of Ireland's leading agriculturalists and Stuart Trench was awarded the silver and gold medal of the Royal Agricultural Society of Ireland'. The onset of the mid-nineteenth-century potato blight put paid to the project, which Joyce describes vividly as 'an entire 162-acre crop creating a horrible stench as it rotted in the ground'.

Reaching the valley lowlands, cross a bridge spanning the Delour River and then go left to reach the outbuildings, which are all that remains of Baunreagh House. Demolished in the 1960s, it is reputed to be Ireland's first dwelling built with concrete. At the time of writing, Baunreagh has been proposed as a trailhead, offering café and bike-hire facilities, for a 40km bike trail which will be linked with a similar 32km bike trail in the

Walk 2: The Central Slieve Bloom

Offaly part of the Slieve Blooms; so it may be a much busier place by the time you get to read this.

At this point you have joined the Slieve Bloom Way, and it is now just a question of following the waymarkers to the right on a diagonally rising, but narrow, track. Turn right on a more defined track and then left on a rough track through forestry, to bring you to the R440 at a stile. Here, the helpful arrows point right along the road to Gorteenameale.

The Slieve Blooms in summer finery.

WALK 3:
Arderin

Grade:	2/3
Time:	45 minutes
Ascent:	80m
Distance:	1.5km
Map:	OSi *Discovery* Series sheet 54

Start & Finish: From the Laois village of Camross or the Offaly village of Kinnitty, follow the signs for Glendine. Park on the Offaly/Laois border in the small car park at the top of the gap.

Suitability: Some disagreeable underfoot terrain, so boots are required. The path is indistinct, so disorientation possible in mist.

Modest in stature, even by Irish standards, the Slieve Blooms are an unpretentious group of eminences. Unlike other Leinster ranges such as the Cooley and Wicklow Mountains, they have mostly remained aloof and secluded as Irish history ebbed and flowed, not so much over them as around them. They did, however, provide a convenient redoubt from which the Gaelic O'Moore and O'Carroll clans resisted the Tudor plantation of Laois and Offaly and thereby ensured this endeavour was but a minimal success. After the far more successful – from an English point of view – Cromwellian plantation of the seventeenth century, the Blooms became relatively peaceful, occupied by increasing numbers of Irish-speaking, Catholic tenant farmers. Mostly paying rent to English-speaking landlords based in the surrounding lowlands, these mountainy folk appear to have been relatively accepting of their lot, showing little evidence of the rebellious nature that characterised those residing in many other parts of Ireland.

The majestically titled Arderin ('Height of Ireland') is the uppermost point of the range and was once inexplicably regarded by some as Ireland's loftiest mountain. Actually, it is just half the height of Carrauntoohil, with its main claim to notoriety coming from its location close to an ancient

Walk 3: Arderin

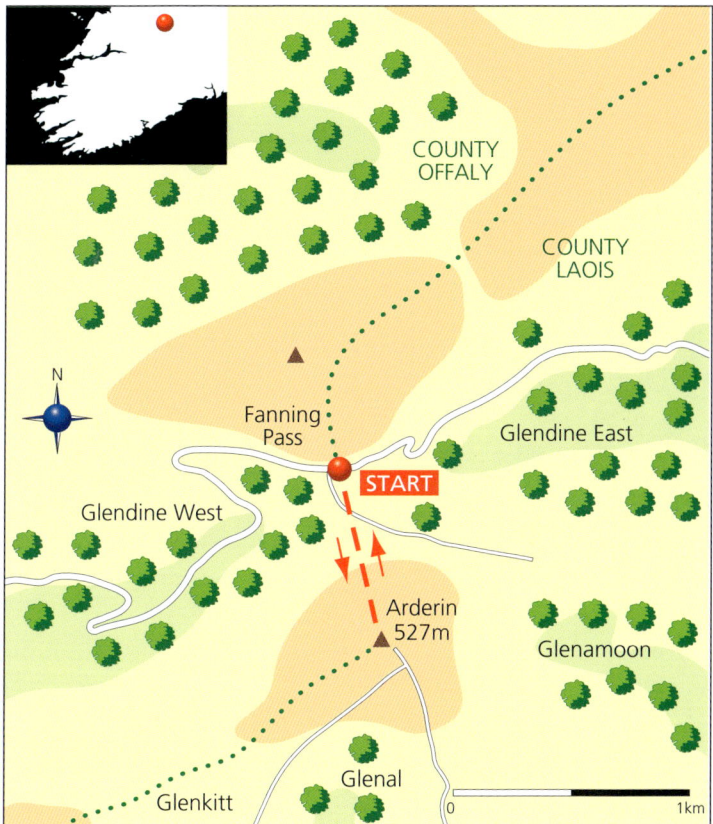

bridle path over the Glendine Gap. In prehistoric times, this made it a suitably central location for the mystical celebrations and overindulgences associated with the Festival of Lughnasa.

An isolated summit, it required a considerable effort to reach until relatively recently. For many a peak bagger, this served as a handy excuse for non-completion until a road built in the 1990s, following an ancient *Slí* through the Glendine Gap, removed this pretext. Now the route has become a regular objective for those completing the Irish County High Points – the 27 highest points in each of the 32 counties of Ireland (some counties share the same high point). The mountain has also given its name to 'the Arderins', the a list of Irish hills having an elevation of 500m or above and with a drop of at least 30m on all sides. A considerable amount of summit visitations come from individuals completing these lists, as the mountain is itself an Arderin.

Glendine East.

The journey upwards through the Glendine Gap is breathtakingly isolated, when you approach from either the Laois or Offaly side, with great declivities tumbling below, which will leave you in no doubt as to why Glendine translates from the Irish language as 'deep glen'. Your start point **S230 996** lies on the boundary between Glendine East and Glendine West, both of which are now heavily forested but which, as late as the early twentieth century, supported substantial populations. The greater proportion was in the western valley, then located in King's County (Offaly). This also marks the border between Laois and Offaly and is known as the J.I. Fanning Pass, in commemoration of Jim Fanning, editor of the Birr-based *Midland Tribune* newspaper and the founder, in 1972, of the Slieve Bloom Association.

Rather incongruously, your ascent of Arderin starts as a steep descent into a little ravine, after which you follow a muddy track uphill taking the right-hand option at a divide in the route. As you plod through the uneven, heathery terrain, you may be reminded of the benefit that upland farming provides for ramblers. The blanket bogs of the high Slieve Blooms are Ireland's largest state-owned nature reserve and are managed by the National Parks and Wildlife Service to ensure the conservation of this ecosystem. The downside is that there is now no livestock. Sheep, and indeed feral goats, control heather by eating it and creating trails that ease the passage of walkers. In the Comeraghs, Knockmealdowns and Galtees,

Arderin, viewed from the J.I. Fanning Pass.

you may notice how rough grazing in upland commonages makes rambling generally easier when compared with the foot-snagging, knee-jarring terrain of the livestock-free Blooms.

In about 25 minutes you are on the summit, which is marked by a small cairn and buried trig pillar and represents, at 527m, the highest point for counties Laois and Offaly. Clearly, the whaleback mountaintop offered plenty of space for the singing, dancing and merrymaking associated with the ancient festival of Lughnasa, although you may wonder how much the heathery terrain hindered these festivities. Otherwise, the immediate surroundings are a tad underwhelming, for the reward hereabouts lies with distance. In *Bladhma* (1995) Tom Joyce quotes one J. Baldwin as stating in 1819 that, 'The view from the Heights of Ireland comprises 15 counties, and is perhaps the most extensive and richest in Ireland.' Whether this is true or not, Arderin certainly gifts an all-embracing panorama, for there are few highlands nearby to circumvent the vista.

The most important rule to remember about Arderin is, however, that you stray beyond the summit at your peril: egregious boot-capturing bog lurks beneath many temptingly green swards. There is also the fact that the surrounding glens have been densely planted with commercial timber, which acts like a series of Berlin Walls to block access. An old and rough farm path does lead almost directly south through to Glenal, but since this runs through private farmland the permission of the owner should be obtained before using it. This is probably not worth the effort unless you have transport pre-arranged from Glenal. Otherwise, you face the prospect of a 9km uphill slog on tarmac to regain the head of the J.I. Fanning Pass. Another option is to follow a path south and then east beside a drainage channel to the head of Glenmoon, but here you will have to descend through difficult woodland to gain the forestry service roadway, which leads easily back to the Glendine Pass road.

For most, however, the prudent course of action will involve the retracing of steps back to the J.I. Fanning Pass. While doing this you will most likely conclude that the 'Height of Ireland' is for a clear day when the half-of-Ireland vista offers just reward for unsympathetic terrain.

View east from the Arderin summit.

WALK 4:
The Eastern Slieve Bloom

Grade:	2/3
Time:	5 hours
Ascent:	355m
Distance:	20km
Map:	OSi *Discovery* Series sheet 54

Start & Finish: From Mountrath, County Laois, follow the signs for the Slieve Bloom Mountains and then Clonaslee. Park at Monicknew car park.

Suitability: a mostly unchallenging circuit offering much walker-friendly terrain but including some tedious moorland, so wear boots. The route is fully waymarked with walking arrows for the Slieve Bloom Way.

It seems that, in the past, people rarely ventured into the Slieve Blooms. No great heroic myths or tales of epic battles have emanated from here. No enormous burial cairns adorn the highest mountaintops. A Kevin, Finbarr or Columba never chanced this way to found a secluded monastic settlement that would draw the faithful from succeeding generations into this great fastness. Lead, silver or gold in sufficient quantities to create a mining boom just didn't exist.

The Victorian bridge at Monicknew

We can safely surmise, therefore, that for most of human history the more elevated areas of the Blooms remained an almost completely pristine wilderness, the lonesome realm of the wolf packs and wild boar. It was a rapidly increasing population in the eighteenth century that forced people upwards to try and eke a living from these unforgiving uplands. For a brief period, in the eighteenth and

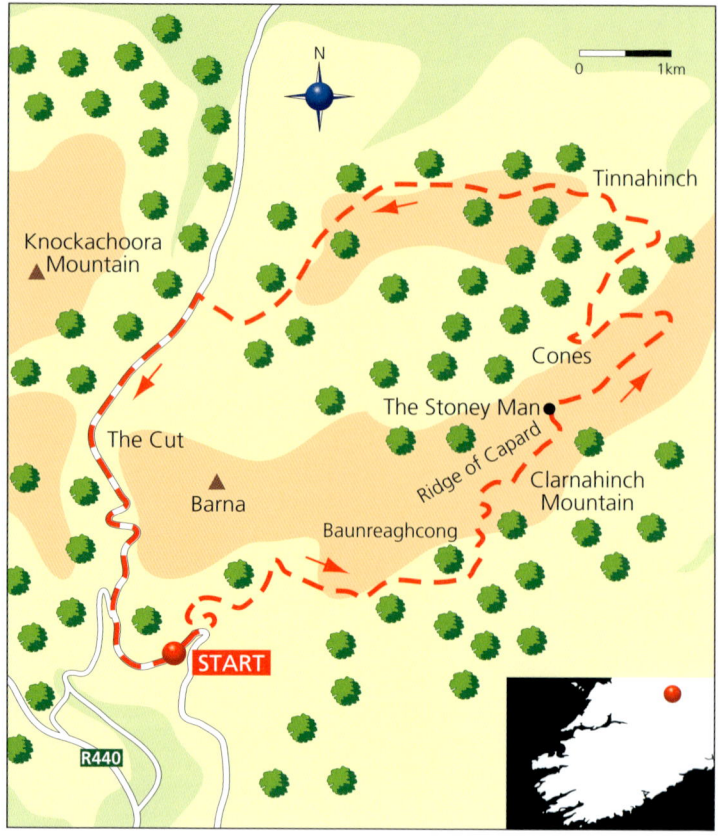

nineteenth centuries, the Blooms supported a relatively large population. In the end, however, it was potato blight that irrevocably put an end to this dense pattern of land settlement.

The Great Irish Famine, which cost the lives of 1 million people, did not hit the east to the extent that it devastated western parts of Ireland. A more robust and diversified economy ensured this, but Queen's County (Laois) was the worst-affected area in Leinster. Here, we must assume that the hardest hit were the tenant farmers of the Slieve Blooms, who would have been most dependent on the potato, because of its ability to return high yields from relatively poor acidic soils. As evidence for this, a famine-relief road was built on Wolftrap Mountain to provide employment for the destitute. Like so many other such endeavours it ended up leading precisely nowhere: back-breaking work by a starving people for no purpose. Certainly, it comes as no surprise that steep, post-famine population decline saw large numbers of families leave the Blooms never

Walk 4: The Eastern Slieve Bloom

The footbridge over the River Barrow.   *The Cut.*

to return; this meant much arduously reclaimed land quickly rewilded to its original state.

And here is one of the great attractions of exploring the Blooms today: the sense of being away from it all in a natural wilderness. Another advantage that may surprise you is the comparatively dry climate. Rainfall levels are on average only about half of the mean annual rainfall for the Kerry Mountains; you don't get lakes, but you do have a much better chance of rambling over a sunlit upland.

To enjoy a genuine backcountry experience, start from Monicknew, which is accessed by an impressively tall single-arch, Victorian-era bridge over the Glen River. From Monicknew car park, **N306 023,** follow the yellow arrows for the Slieve Bloom Way past a picnic table and along a gravel path that, in the month of May, leads through a profusion of flowering bluebells. Join a forest track, go right and then right again along a green lane. Continue uphill through mixed woodland above the Glen River to gain a forest clearing. A right-hand turn here takes you across the busy headwaters of the Glen to a forestry road, where we go left. Expansive views now open across rolling highlands as you reach the top of the hill and then begin descending the southern shoulder of Baunreaghcong Mountain with a sense of spaciousness all around.

Back on level terrain, the way is left and upwards on a dogleg track before ascending through a forest break and going right along the boggy flanks of Clarnahinch Mountain. A horse-racing aficionado would probably describe the going as 'yielding to soft' but at least it is relieved, in places, by the addition of a boardwalk. Eventually the route swings left and upwards to gain the redoubt of the Stoney Man.

This perfectly symmetrical cairn is probably the best-known man-made object in the Blooms and was built as a waymarker during a time when quarrying was carried on extensively in the area. The Ridge of Capard now beckons north-eastwards along its rough, heathery crest. Come to a boardwalk; the way is left and left again on a track leading downhill through a gate. Soon after, the lachrymose remains of several ruined cottages provide a glimpse to the past. These once formed the little village of Cones, which was populated by the Fitzpatrick, Lawlor, Clear and Conroy families. Attached to the outer wall of the best-preserved house you will notice a plaque to the memory of Anne Clear who, in 1962, became the last person to abandon the unequal struggle with the mountainside and leave the glen.

Life would certainly have been harsh and isolated here, particularly in winter. In his book, *Bladhma*, Tom Joyce recounts that in the great freeze of 1947, the snow was up to the eaves of this cottage and neighbours had to dig the family out to rescue them. The harshness did not, however, prevent the long arm of landlordism reaching the area with the tenant farmers of Cones obliged to pay annual rent to the Piggott family of Capard House. Times were also tough for children, required each day to make a crossing of the Ridge of Capard to and from school.

It's downhill now to go right at a sharp bend and then follow a gravel track leading to the bank of the infant River Barrow. Local mythology dictates the source of the River Barrow to be a spring known as 'the Well of Slieve Bloom', which is located on Barna Mountain. Tradition holds that if anyone dares to touch or even gaze upon these emergent waters, the well will immediately overflow in a great torrent to inundate the low-lying lands below. Those living downstream will, however, be relieved to learn that nobody in modern times has managed to pinpoint exactly the location of this fabled fountain.

Following the Barrow downstream brings you to a sturdy footbridge which conveys you across to an area known as Tinnahinch. Initially follow the riverbank downstream before breaking left to ascend steeply through mixed and not very dense woodland to arrive at a forest roadway. The way here lies directly west on forest roadway with occasional vistas opening to Ireland's boggy central lowlands. Beyond a forest barrier, a boardwalk gives access to an area on the left that has been preserved as a nature reserve for the original blanket bog. Invading conifers have been removed to prevent the bog from drying out and natural drainage ditches blocked to recreate its naturally saturated state.

If you have done your preparation well, you will have pre-positioned a car or a bicycle at this point or, perhaps, arranged for a friend to pick you up. Failing this, it is left along the quiet Mountrath/Clonaslee road which leads generally south through 'the Cut' and then onwards for about 4km to reach Monicknew.

WALK 5:
Giant's Grave and the Spink

Grade:	2
Time:	4 hours
Ascent:	240m
Distance:	14km
Map:	OSi *Discovery* Series sheet 54

Start & Finish: This walk begins in Cadamstown village, which lies on the R421/R422 between Clonaslee, County Laois and Kinnitty, County Offaly. Park beside Dempsey's Pub.

Suitability: Relatively unchallenging if rather extended outing that explores isolated upland terrain while offering the navigational comfort of laneways, paths and forest tracks, throughout. Care required on the path above the Silver River.

Historians and Gaelic scholars have not been able to establish a consensus about what *Sliabh Bladhma* (the Irish name for the Slieve Blooms) refers to. It is, however, an almost universal truism that every self-respecting mountain range comes with a tale of a mythological hero who roamed its summits and the Blooms are no exception. Where historic fact leaves a gap, mythology will inevitably fill the vacuum and so local tradition holds the Blooms have been named in honour of a mythical warrior called Bladhma. To interrogate this legend further, set out from Cadamstown (**N227 085**) and follow arrows uphill along an old coach road passing by a rustic track known locally as Paul's Lane. The shorter and easier Paul's Lane Loop (marked with blue arrows) goes right here and offers you a rewarding two-hour alternative if time is short.

Otherwise, continue straight ahead until a finger sign for 'Giant's Grave' points right. Follow the tarmac gently uphill and then go past a barrier to gain a forest road. Ignore the first junction to the right and, soon after, an arrow for 'Giant's Grave' points left through woodland. Cross a footbridge to arrive at a clearing where the megalithic tomb known as the Giant's Grave is located.

   Initially it will probably appear a rather unimpressive if pleasant site, since it was virtually destroyed by eighteenth-century tomb raiders who apparently were rewarded for their vandalism with the discovery of a golden spur. All that marks the location now is a group of scattered boulders that once formed the burial chamber, within which, local tradition holds, the eponymous Bladhma was interred. Originally from west of the Shannon, he is reputed to have killed an important chief and afterwards fled to the sanctuary of the Slieve Blooms. Here, he became the local strongman for a period before eventually being slain in battle.

   Beyond the Giant's Grave the path joins the Slieve Bloom Way. Go right here and right again when you reach a four-way junction where the Slieve Bloom Way departs left. After about 100m, swing left at a point where the Slieve Bloom Way reappears and tag it along a forestry track leading gently uphill to reach a clear area near the summit of Spink Mountain that offers superb views. Here you will behold the big skies over Ireland's central plain to the north while to the south lies secluded Glendineoregan, framed by the extensive moorland plateau of Wolftrap Mountain.

Walk 5: Giant's Grave and the Spink

The Giant's Grave

Parting from the Slieve Bloom Way once again, it is onwards now past two gateways. Then a lovely sweeping descent leads to a three-way junction where you veer right and again rejoin the Slieve Bloom Way, which continues its game of hide-and-seek with the route. Follow the forestry road to a point where it turns left on a narrow path through a clear-felled forest where tree stumps have been cleverly used to mark the route. To the left the landscape slopes away into a series of small fields as a poignant ode to the era before the indigenous population were driven back by an incoming tide of Sitka spruce and Norwegian pine. Exit this path at a small streamlet known as Purcell's Book.

Cross the tiny brook and turn left onto an old laneway where you join with the Paul's Lane Loop for a joint return to Cadamstown. The laneway leads downhill to reach a gateway at a captivating weir on the Silver River, which on a sunny day makes a lovely place to linger amid the sound of hurrying waters.

Beyond, a stile leads to a spectacular path overlooking the Silver River. Unchained by rising temperatures from the great glaciers that once banked against the northern side of the Blooms, meltwaters carved a spectacularly deep gorge in the sandstone here and in some places exposing the underlying Silurian rock.

Coming to a point where a sign declares 'Sheep Rock Face, Keep Out' you will be confronted by the idiosyncratic nature of the Irish personality; a path has, of course, been worn away to investigate the forbidden. The hurrying waters now descend over biscuit-box cascades and eddies which can be viewed from a convenient wooden bridge spanning the river. This is also a good place to marvel at how past floods managed to convey

Looking south towards Wolftrap Mountain.

such almighty boulders downstream and an excellent location to observe the layering in a nearby cliff, which is a feature of how sandstone rock formations are laid down.

Abandoning the river, the path ascends to a wooden stile accessing farmland. Turning left into a bucolic laneway will then take you downhill and through a concrete stile to the trailhead. Here, you will most likely conclude that, well-managed and promoted like the English Peak District, which draws millions of annual visitors, the Slieve Bloom area has clear potential to become Ireland's playground for ramblers seeking gentler outings with plenty to enthrall along the way.

Weir on the Silver River.

Upperchurch village.

The Slievefelim Hills

You have been a low-level walker for some time and your fitness has improved. Now that you're ready to move on and a little voice is murmuring, 'what next?' you know these voices can only be silenced by more of a challenge – capturing your very own mountaintop, perhaps – but you are not ready yet for navigating the often-trackless moorland of the high Galtees and Comeraghs.

Don't let this be a worry, for in these circumstances you can find just the challenge you want amid the captivating charm of the – until recently – little-known Slievefelim Hills. The attraction of these gentle north Tipperary uplands is that, compared with their south-county counterparts, they are on a different, more intimate scale and do not make the less-experienced walker feel insignificant or out of place. The Slievefelim are a patchwork of small fields, woodlands, serene villages and moorland tops and an area where a strong sense of localism still flourishes among the inhabitants. Humans fit in naturally even on the highest summits, which are reached by well-marked trails through a landscape littered with abundant historic artefacts to capture your curiosity and stretch your imagination.

WALK 6:
The Eamonn a Chnoic Loop

Grade:	2
Time:	2½ hours
Ascent:	150m
Distance:	8km
Map:	OSi *Discovery* Series sheet 59

Start & Finish: From Thurles, County Tipperary, follow the R498 (Nenagh road) for about 2km. At a junction for Limerick take the R503 for 13km to a crossroads with a fingerpost (right) for Upperchurch. The trailhead is located in the village about 500m from here.

Suitability: Moderate outing traversing minor roads, laneways and fields, which can be muddy in places so walking boots are essential. The walk crosses worked agricultural land, so leave the dog at home, do not disturb farm animals and generally try to minimise your environmental footprint.

Our most compelling landscapes are not necessarily the most pristine and unaltered. Indeed, the Irish countryside can be at its most captivating where it works hardest for a living. Nowhere is this more apparent than in the landscape north of Upperchurch, County Tipperary, where an innovative approach to recreational walking in Ireland was originally piloted. With freedom of access granted by 23 local farmers, this easy but captivating loop meanders through wildflower-rich meadows of working farms and rustic bridleways filled with birdsong and the evocative aromas of the countryside.

Following a rural lane towards Mokeland.

Walk 6: The Eamonn a Chnoic Loop

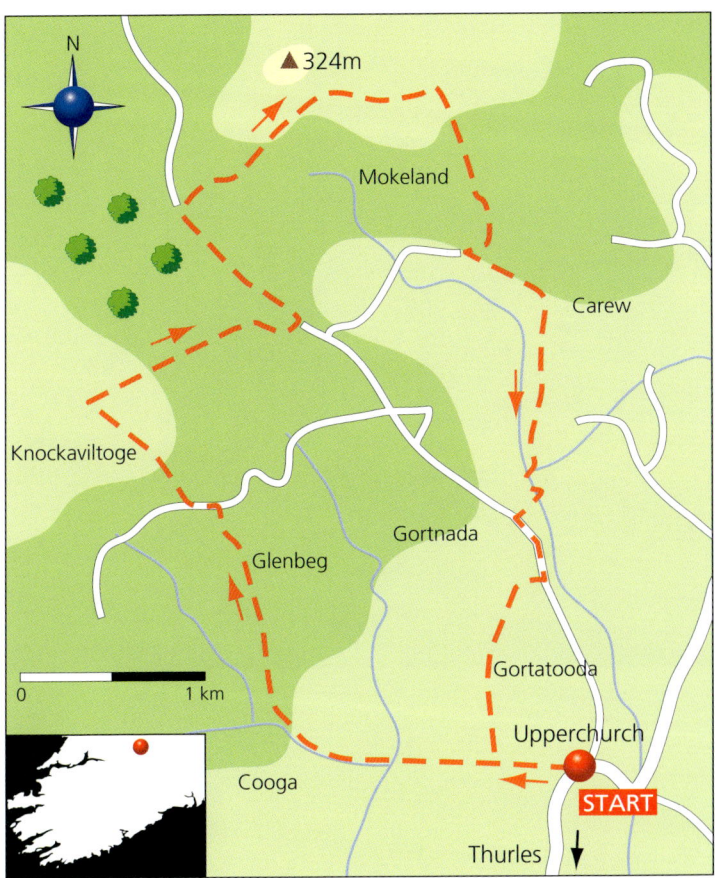

This is a corner of Ireland where the environmental mischief-making of past EU agricultural policies never really built a head of steam. The timeless landscape of small fields, luxuriant hedgerows and diverse habitats has somehow survived the onslaught of globalised food production. And if you wish to make it so, this area can be a true wellspring for the imagination, for with just a small step of imagining, mountainy men are once again working the fields with horse-drawn ploughs while cows stand placid and content to be hand-milked on summer evenings. Certainly, it is a peaceful environment where a chance encounter with a local is a welcome event. Treat it as an opportunity to discover something about the rich folklore of the area and the renowned Upperchurch welcome will be yours for the taking.

Eamonn a Chnoic was an Upperchurch-born rapparee named Edmund O'Ryan. In the Robin Hood tradition, he is reputed to have robbed wealthy

Imbibing of the pastoral expanse below Mokeland.

English planters to assist the Irish poor and is still celebrated locally by a sombre ballad of dispossession. To follow the loop that honours his name, take the road from the trailhead in Upperchurch village (**R987 612**) that passes the community centre and a childcare facility. After about ten minutes you reach a bridge. Just beyond, use the small gate on your right to enter a field and climb through a series of meadows with linking stiles through areas known as Cooga and Glenbeg. At the crest of the ascent you emerge on a roadway and go left.

After 100m, divert right onto a track and then cross a stile to join a green road that leads into a field. Then go right and left to exit the field over a stile and join a bucolic laneway where a sign informs you that this was once the location of a hedge school where the teacher's name was Bourke.

Following the dissolution of the Irish monasteries in the sixteenth century, hedge schools were a valuable source of education for the rural poor. Later, when Catholic schools were officially banned under the Penal Laws, they were the only avenue to education for those Catholic families, who could not afford to send their children for education abroad. Hedge schools persisted until well into the nineteenth century when they were supplanted by the coming of free primary education.

The lane now conveys you downhill by the right-hand side of a house to a public road where you go left, following the tarmac for 300m before swinging right at a small hay barn. Now enjoy the splendid quietude of the upland countryside as you tag a green road until the route crosses a stile and hugs the edge of a plantation. Nearing the end of the trees turn right and descend by following the walking arrows through a series of fields, in an area known locally as Mokeland, to reach yet another laneway.

Cross this lane and then traverse several more fields and a couple of tiny steams before exiting onto a public road where the way is left. After 100m the walking signs point to a laneway on the right. Now it is plain trailing all the way as you cross a stile and continue through a field to reach Church Bog, which has been developed by the local community as a wildlife habitat, accessible walking trail and Mecca for overseas tourists wishing to enjoy turf-cutting demonstrations.

Leave the bog via a gate to the public road, turn left and enjoy a pleasant 300m stroll back to the warm hospitality of three-pub Upperchurch village.

Returning to Upperchurch village.

WALK 7:
Keeper Hill (Slievekimalta)

Grade:	2/3
Time:	3½ hours
Ascent:	550m
Distance:	14km
Map:	OSi *Discovery* Series sheet 59

Start & Finish: From the Tipperary village of Newport take the road signposted Nenagh. After a short distance, swing right at a graveyard and continue to a crossroads where a fingerpost for Keeper Trailhead points left. Follow a series of these signs on small roads to Doonane car park.

Suitability: Route follows well-maintained tracks. Venture off track, however, and the terrain often becomes challenging.

The highest mountain in the Shannon region presides over an area where communities have, for centuries, displayed a doughty independence, attracting rebels and writers in equal measure. Keeper Hill looked down impassively as the seventeenth-century rapparee Michael Galloping Hogan passed beneath at the head of Patrick Sarsfield's men, on an audacious, but successful, mission to destroy a Limerick-bound siege train with a cargo of large cannon.

It watched Eamonn a Chnoic – a local-born outlaw – sally forth on a one-man mission to improve social cohesion by forcefully transferring income from haves to have-nots. He also reputedly found time to pen the epic poem 'Seán Ó Duibhir an Ghleanna' and remains the only Irish outlaw to be commemorated with a memorial, which now stands at Curraheen near Hollyford village.

And it was in the last century that writer and uncompromising revolutionary Ernie O'Malley slipped into Keeper's shadow at the head of Munster's 2nd Southern Division, IRA. Here, he led attacks by local activists on the nearby Hollyford and Rearcross RIC Barracks and at one time commanded 7,000 volunteers in the area.

Walk 7: Keeper Hill (Slievekimalta)

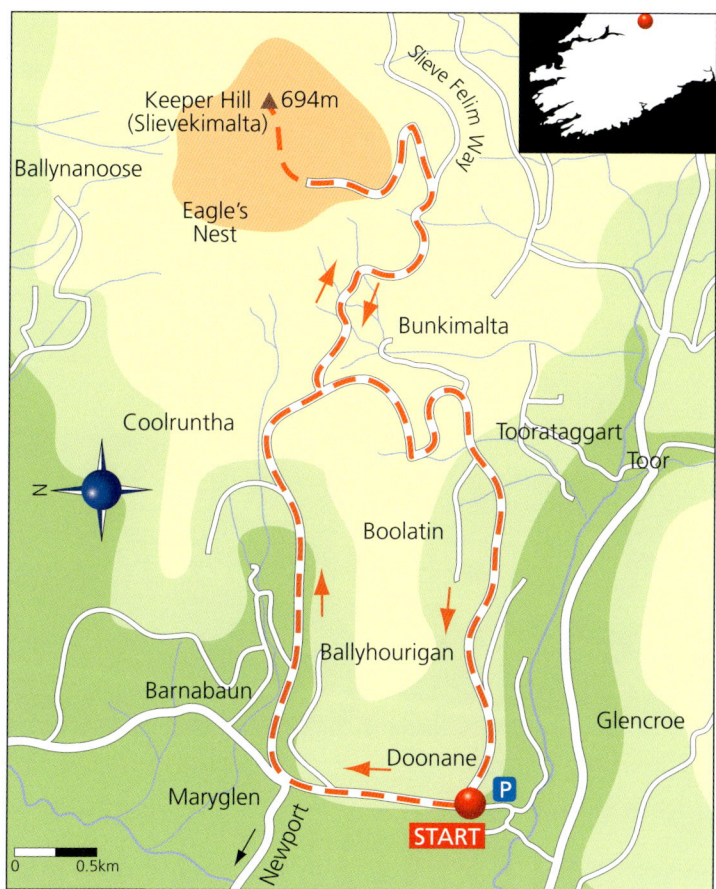

These days Slievefelim is more famous for the enduring strength and vibrancy of its community initiatives with people also coming year-round to avail of an excellent network of trails developed by admirable local enterprise. Sooner or later, however, most visitors will be drawn to the great whaleback mountain that towers imperiously above the surrounding hills. Despite this impressive outline and 694m altitude, Keeper is actually a rather benign beast.

The ascent can prove physically demanding, but otherwise it represents 'hillwalking-lite' as the summit is accessed by a reassuringly well-marked track.

Your walk to the summit of Keeper Hill starts from the well-appointed Doonane car park **R781 652** (see panel above) where you follow the red arrows uphill for about 1.5km to Ballyhourigan Wood. Here, you follow the

Keeper Hill.

forest track east for about 3km until it swings south beneath a prominent outcrop known as the Eagle's Nest to reach a three-way junction.

Join the Slievefelim Way by taking the left-hand option and continue beneath an eye-catching gully and then a serene waterfall before the trail begins contouring the south face of the mountain.

When the forest clears on the right, immense vistas will open over the tiny village of Toor, with a line of low hills farther south and, beyond these, the great sweep of the Galtee Mountains.

Soon afterwards, you will part company with the Slievefelim Way by following the red walking arrows upwards to the left. This much-improved path now leads to the summit by a circuitous, but not overly steep, route. Along the way there are glimpses of Slievenamon, the Blackstairs Range and the distant Wicklow Mountains.

The summit of Keeper Hill (694m) contains the almost obligatory cairn and trig point along with a huge and decidedly non-obligatory communication mast. The intoxicating vista over the north Tipperary hills to the distant Slieve Bloom Mountains provides adequate compensation, however, for such intrusion.

Descend initially by the same route and then, on a clear day with the vegetation thickening once again you will notice to the west an arc of distant hills. You may initially wonder as to the location of these ranges and then be surprised to figure out that these mountains are in faraway west Cork and Kerry. First to enter your line of vision will most likely be the somewhat suggestive shape of the Paps Mountains. Then further west you will spy Mangerton, and next the unmistakably angular peaks of the MacGillycuddy's Reeks. The Slievemish lie further north and beyond, and seemingly isolated in the silvery western ocean is the sharp outline of the Brandon Ridge.

Good underfoot conditions on the route to the summit of Keeper Hill.

Eventually you must drag yourself away from the view and descend to the three-way junction encountered earlier. Now follow the blue arrows of the Ballyhourigan Loop instead of retracing your steps to Ballyhourigan Wood, for easy going on a well-signed trail with the fertile patchwork of the renowned Golden Vale laid out below.

When you reach a three-way junction, swing left for the short stroll downhill to Doonane while perhaps reflecting on the relative insignificance of our island where even innocuous Keeper Hill offers vistas that encompass virtually the entire south of Ireland.

Wildflowers adorning the flanks of Keeper Hill.

WALK 8:
The Knockalough Loop

Grade:	2/3
Time:	3 hours
Ascent:	320m
Distance:	10km
Map:	OSi *Discovery* Series sheet 66

Start & Finish: From Thurles take the R498 Nenagh road for 2km. At the junction, signposted Limerick, take the R503 and continue for about 13km to a crossroads with a fingerpost (right) for Upperchurch. Go left instead and you will come to the Knockalough trailhead after about 500m. There are parking opportunties at the large forest entrance here.

Suitability: Completing the Knockalough Loop is reasonably strenuous as loop walks go and is also fully exposed to the elements in places. So, bring warm clothing and raingear, follow the purple arrows and do not stray from the marked route.

Communities, it is often said, are dense networks of human interactions accompanied by a strong sense of place and certainly there seems to be something in the air around the tiny parish of Upperchurch that breeds altruistic endeavour. For decades now, a group of individuals has worked tirelessly and unremunerated to make the area a byword for proactive rural development. Latterly they have been justly rewarded, with 'Brand Upperchurch' acquiring a muscular appeal that attracts improbably large numbers of visitors for even innocuous local events. One result of this unstinting local endeavour is that this tiny upland community now boasts four excellent walking trails with each telling a different story.

Of these, the Knockalough Loop reaches the highest elevation and offers an opportunity to walk arm-in-arm with the ghosts of history, for this is an area associated with the tragic southward journey of Red Hugh O'Donnell – the last of the great Ulster chieftains. Having escaped from

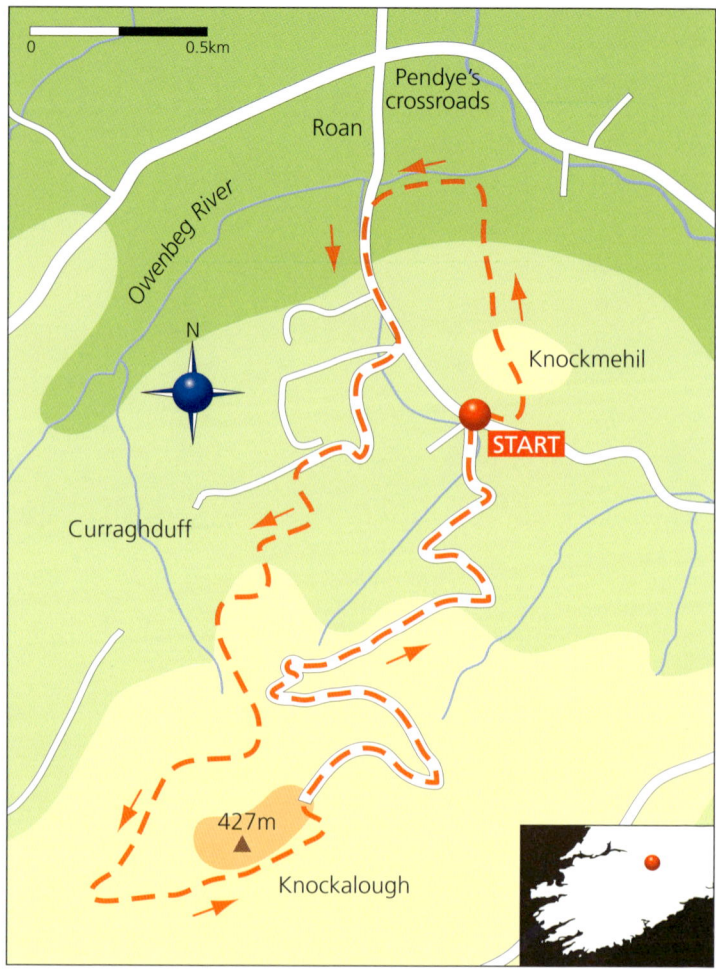

captivity in Dublin Castle during the severe winter of 1592, O'Donnell immediately instigated a rebellion against English rule in Ireland. In 1601, he chanced this way on his heroic but ultimately catastrophic march to defeat at the Battle of Kinsale that forever ended Ireland's Gaelic way of life.

Starting the Knockalough Loop from the forestry entrance at **R988 596**, cross the road and climb the stile, following the purple arrows. The first section of the loop takes you through pleasant pastures to exit at a surfaced road where you turn left. Follow the surfaced road to reach the entrance to a farmyard on your right.

Panoramic view of Knockalough.

From here keep right of a farm building and continue for about 600m on a farm roadway to reach a stile on your left where you enter a field and ascend. At the corner of the field go right and follow the hedge to the next corner where you turn left and climb again. After 100m you turn right at two gates – crossing a stile and joining a rustic trail alongside a forestry plantation. Follow this to reach a stile at the entrance to a wood. Now ascend steeply by the edge of woodland to exit onto a forestry service road where you turn right.

Follow this roadway around the edge of forestry as it runs close by but does not actually bring you to the summit proper (427m), which is secreted in woodland. Nevertheless, marvellous views open here to the west across the bewitching expanse of the Slievefelim highlands to the crowning glories of Mauherslieve and Keeper Hill adorning the western horizon.

Walkers ascend Knockalough.

Walk 8: The Knockalough Loop

View over Upperchurch village to the north Tipperary hills.

Eventually, the blue walking arrows will point right, but if you feel you have had sufficient exercise for one day, you may continue straight ahead. This will bring you to a well-surfaced forest roadway where you will then regain the blue walking arrows and follow these left and downhill for just over 2km to reach your start point. This will reduce the overall length of the walk by 2km and 90m of ascent.

Otherwise, go right and soon after left over a stile and pursue the arrows on a dogleg trail that descends steeply in places. This takes you to a shallow, grassy ravine which you follow left and upwards. At the top, the arrows point left and uphill along a forest edge. A wooden stile leads to a forest roadway beyond which you merely tag the blue arrows downhill for about 2.5km to regain the trailhead.

Mahon Falls.

The Comeragh Mountains

Ultimately it is geology that creates the ever-changing template that makes hillwalking such an enthralling pastime. This is particularly true in Ireland where the landscape displays an amazing geological diversity, given the size of the island. The limestone pavements of the Burren give way to the quartzite hills of Connemara, and then the ancient metamorphic rocks of Donegal melt into the newer volcanic basalts of Antrim. Granite dominates our eastern hills before once again conceding to the startlingly different old sandstones of the south-west's mountains.

And it is this process of transformation that gives a distinctly edgy feel to the Comeragh Mountains, for these are uplands in transition. It is here that the sharper outlines, thunderous cliffs and immense glacial corries that bite hungrily into the Comeragh Plateau replace the gentler, rounded Leinster hills as a precursor to the raw, untamed peaks of the south-west.

So, if your rambles have to date been confined to Ireland's east coast, you will doubtless be delighted to discover that the Comeragh Mountains provide an easily accessible walking experience comparable with the best on offer anywhere in Ireland.

WALK 9:
The Nire Valley Coums

Grade: 4
Time: 5 hours
Ascent: 790m
Distance: 15km
Map: OSi *Discovery* Series sheet 75

Start & Finish: From Clonmel, take the R671 Dungarvan road to the County Waterford village of Ballymacarberry. Turn left at Melody's pub and continue until you reach a thatched house at a junction lying beside a scenic bridge. From here a narrow road leads right for about 4km to reach the Nire Valley car park.

Suitability: A challenging outing suitable for fit, well-equipped walkers. In mist, precise navigation skills are required on the featureless Comeragh Plateau.

Despite the environmental mischief created by a decade of largely unregulated economic growth, it is still possible to uncover places where the Celtic Tiger failed to leave a calling card. Waterford's Nire Valley is one example, for this elevated landscape remains rural and appealing, but not in the extravagantly touristy way of pretty footbridges, tea shops, kissing gates and story-boarded viewing points.

Immutable through countless generations, the Nire is instead a jumbled patchwork of sheep pens, small fields, stone walls and improvised fencing – in fact, all the real-life monuments from times when subsistence incomes were hard won from unforgiving mountainsides. The remoteness of the area was undoubtedly a factor in its choice as the location for the final meeting of the IRA Army Council to take place during the Irish Civil war. The attendance at this March 1923 meeting, in the farmhouse of John Wall, included such notables as Éamon de Valera, Tom Barry, Frank Aiken and IRA commander Liam Lynch, who would soon after die in combat on the slopes of the nearby Knockmealdown Mountains.

Even today there is a palpable feeling about the area of detachment from modernity. Visitors are most welcome but will find themselves in a go-as-you-find-it landscape that could double as a film set depicting the unrelenting toil of nineteenth-century upland living.

To begin your exploration of these memorable moorlands, park in the Nire Valley car park **S276 128** (see panel above). Now follow the arrows for the Nire Lakes along a driveway where a sign banning dogs is a reminder that the local economy is heavily dependent on sheep farming.

What most walkers do not realise, however, is that these animals also steward the uplands, maintaining biodiversity by controlling the spread

The Nire Valley .

of bracken and heather. Any downturn in the viability of upland farming caused by the globalisation of agricultural production should therefore be a concern for hillwalkers. Such a decline would not only endanger the viability of upland communities but would also, by removing the benefit of close-grazing sheep, threaten to transform mountain walking from recreational pleasure to heathery torment.

Next go through a gateway and continue a short distance before swinging left by the rear of a farmhouse to reach another gateway leading to open mountain. A steep descent to the right now leads to a stream in a deep gorge. Cross with care, particularly when water levels are high, before continuing roughly south, towards a broad spur marking the western extent of the Nire coums.

Every mountain range holds a bank of secrets, and the Comeraghs are no exception. The spur offers a gentle ascent and brings you to a lonesome plateau where the true glory of the area is revealed. Now it is clear that the Comeragh Mountains resemble a huge half-eaten trifle with a series of lake-strewn coums scooped into the massive flanks.

Easy walking and spectacular views now follow on a track above Coumfea and Coumalocha. When the clifftop route eventually swings east it is worth diverting the short distance south to the rim above Coumtay for

The Comeragh coums.

a breathtaking vista over an extravagant tapestry of great cliffs and gullies to the Waterford lowlands and the south coast beyond.

Returning to Coumalocha, you continue contouring the clifftop before heading directly north until you encounter steep ground above the Sgilloge Loughs. Contour right here until you arrive at a stream that topples spectacularly over the clifftop.

When the wind blows directly into this coum it carries spray backwards from the waterfall to form an unmistakable smoke-like plume, which freezes into wonderfully shaped icicles in winter, causing local residents to comment that 'the old woman is smoking her pipe again'.

Next head north-east, where a short uphill flog will bring you to the head of Coumlara, a slender coum that, unusually for this area, lacks a lake. Cross the stream at the head of Coumlara and continue until you reach a sturdy fence. Follow this fence left as it descends north-west to reach a steep bouldery rib.

Adrenalin junkies will enjoy the challenge of descending this, but most walkers will be glad to know that this obstacle can be easily bypassed on the left.

Now return to the fence and descend steeply into the Comeragh Gap to reach a stile in the fence where a track marking an ancient Mass path and trade route crosses at right angles to the fence. Follow this route left, marked by a series of white poles, as it leads you downhill and then uphill again to reach a gate. From here it is a short but rugged descent to the Nire Valley car park below.

Bog cotton on the Comeragh Plateau.

WALK 10:
The Mahon Falls and Coumtay

Grade:	4
Time:	3½ hours
Ascent:	390m
Distance:	6.5km
Map:	OSi *Discovery* Series sheet 75

Start & Finish: From Carrick-on-Suir, drive south on the R676 towards Dungarvan for about 18km. At Mahon Bridge, go right at a signpost for Mahon Falls and immediately right again. After about 1.5km, turn right and continue through an entrance with a cattle grid. You are now on the 'magic road' and the fairy tree is 150m further along on your left.

Suitability: Be aware that this is quite a challenging walk over sometimes tiring terrain on the elevated and featureless Comeragh Plateau. As always, be well equipped with warm clothing and raingear. Carry a map and compass and understand the route crosses featureless uplands where many have previously become disorientated when mist descended suddenly.

Do you believe the magic went out of life the day you discovered Santa's stocking fillers came, not from Lapland, but more likely from Toyland? If so, never fear, for there still exists in County Waterford a *Bothar Draíochta* ('magic road') that evokes our earliest experiences of spine-tingling wonder when confronted with something that is resolutely beyond our powers of comprehension.

A favour-adorned tree beside the 'magic road'.

Walk 10: The Mahon Falls and Coumtay

To relive such evocative moments, follow the road leading to the Mahon Falls in Waterford's Comeragh Mountains (see panel above). At a point just beyond the entrance gate to the falls and near a solitary favour-adorned thorn bush that stands frail but improbably noteworthy,

The Mahon Falls.

switch off your engine and put your gear shift in neutral. Local tradition claims this is a fairy tree and, as if to emphasise this, you will soon have the disconcerting experience of sitting in a car that is reversing uphill as if being propelled by an energetic team of leprechauns.

Rationally minded killjoys have visited here with surveying equipment and concluded that the 'magic road' is merely an optical illusion. Most visitors will, however, find it hard to believe this physics-defying piece of enchantment is merely an illusion when they observe the astonishing speed at which stationary vehicles are propelled upwards.

Still mulling over the improbability of what you have experienced, continue by following the roadway for about 2km into the increasingly timeless Mahon Valley. Stop at a large parking place **S313 080** where at weekends the solitude is invariably hijacked by family groups, picnickers and casual strollers. From here it's 'shank's mare' all the way, starting with a surfaced footpath leading to the Mahon Falls. The best time to visit is a clear morning following a night of heavy rain when the falls are in full torrent and subsidiary waterfalls will also have blossomed from the surrounding cliffs. When the path peters out, cross the River Mahon (with great care when water levels are high) and ascend steep but easy ground, keeping the cascade on your left.

During this ascent, you will observe the waters thundering down a 17m vertical drop into an improbably shallow pool. Amazingly, Tramore canoeist Michael Reynolds kayaked his way down this torrent and survived, unhurt, to tell the tale. For most people, this will come as one more piece of wonder from the Mahon Valley that is scarcely credible without setting eyes on the unquestionably photogenic evidence. From the top of the falls, continue ascending until it is safe to recross the Mahon River.

Now in welcome solitude, strike out west over the heathery Comeragh Plateau for about 1.5km of gently rising ground. Here the going can be somewhat tedious and you will be forced to climb with regularity into the bed of some (hopefully) dry watercourses. Your efforts are well rewarded,

The Mahon Valley.

however, when you reach the cliffs of Coumfea and experience the breathtaking vista from above this lake-strewn corrie that gazes out over the majestic tablecloth of the renowned Nire Valley.

Now head in a southerly direction from Coumfea and continue until your way is barred by the complex architecture of the great cliffs above Coumtay. Here the view southwards is no less majestic and includes the Waterford coast, Dungarvan Harbour and Helvick Head.

Do not attempt to descend directly into Coumtay since much of the south- and east-facing cliff is sheer and punctuated by treacherous gullies. Instead, move left until the angle of slope eases and it is possible to descend safely into the eastern side of the coum. Now follow downstream by the outfall of the River Tay until you are beside a ruined farmhouse secluded in a clump of trees, which is known locally as Ned Curran's Cottage. Commanding a splendid view over the lowlands, it will immediately be clear that this place was well chosen as a safe house and arms dump during both the Irish War of Independence and the Civil War.

Take the track leading uphill and go left to a gate. Then skirt the side of a forest on a rougher track that leads to a tarmacadam roadway. Follow this left and uphill to your parking place, which is just out of sight beyond the highest point of the roadway.

Coumtay in autumn glory.

WALK 11:
Coumshingaun and Crotty's Lough

Grade:	4
Time:	5 hours
Ascent:	730m
Distance:	12km
Map:	OSi *Discovery* Series sheet 75

Start & Finish: Kilclooney Wood car park is located in County Waterford beside the R676 and close to the midpoint between Carrick-on-Suir and Dungarvan.

Suitability: Even in good weather this is a demanding outing. Carry a map and compass and on the longer walk have at least one person in the group who is fully competent to navigate on the featureless Comeragh Plateau.

Once upon a time in the Comeragh Mountains there lived an outlaw named William Crotty. Defiant role models are important in times when ordinary people feel oppressed by external forces and so it is perhaps unsurprising that after his death Crotty quickly morphed into a quixotic eighteenth-century hero. In the best Robin Hood tradition, he is reputed to have robbed the rich to help the poor, while also, of course, retaining some cash to cover miscellaneous expenses. Local legend holds that, somewhere amid the Comeragh fastness, this hoard still awaits a lucky finder. Indeed, this could be a propitious day as you will now be exploring Waterford's Crotty country, which will give an opportunity to keep a discreet eye out for the glitter of sequestered gold.

Begin by taking a woodland track (west) from Kilclooney Wood car park to join a forestry road. Then follow this (right) past a deflector mast that has been cunningly disguised as a tree until the path crosses a fence to open mountainside. Now, it is upwards through scrubby terrain towards a prominent boulder on the skyline. Here, you will clearly see your

The Comeragh, Galtee, Knockmealdown and Slieve Bloom Mountains: A Walking Guide

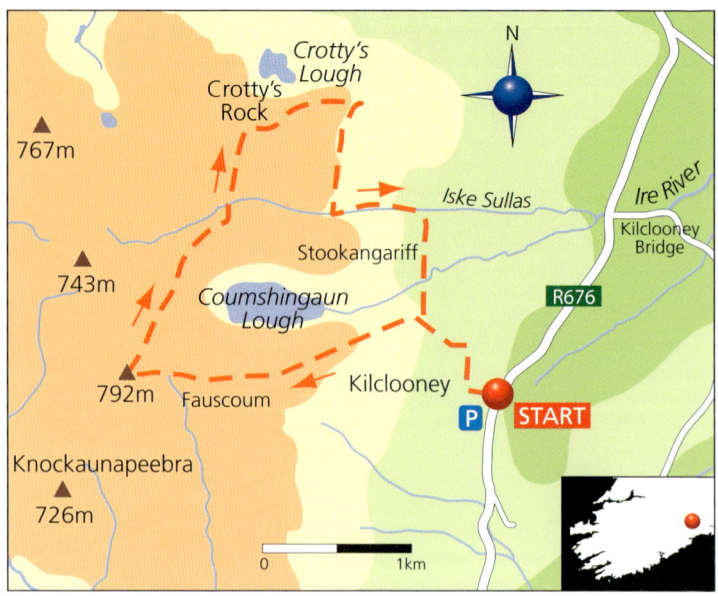

Coumshingaun Lough.

Coumshingaun in springtime.

objective, the ridgeline rising to the left of Coumshingaun. This may seem intimidating and, indeed, it can be a lung-burning challenge, but here is a good place to remember the old rule: if you keep putting one leg in front of the other, every hill will eventually run out of altitude. All you require is sufficient bottle for the shortish battle until the slope eases above majestic Coumshingaun – the largest of the thirteen lakes in the Comeragh Mountains and the finest example of a corrie lake on these islands.

Few clichés remain unhackneyed in describing the glory of Coumshingaun and here the word 'awesome' may immediately spring to mind. Don't worry though, for this is indeed an accurate description when used, not in the modern and diluted sense of something that is just nice or unusual, but rather in the original meaning of a place that genuinely inspires awe. Gazing at the great corrie and the colossal cliffs that guard it, your eye is likely to be drawn towards a substantial rockfall near the north-west corner of the lake. Here, fallen boulders have created a cave system, where, reputedly, Crotty found a hiding place for his horses, all of which had been shod in reverse to confuse pursuing redcoats. This legend may indeed be true as there is plenty of space to hide a pair of equines comfortably under the great east-facing cliffs of the coum. The area also makes an ideal place for family groups wishing to have fun by exploring

On the South Ridge, Coumshingaun.

the many interconnecting caverns of what must have been, at the time of its creation, a most spectacular rockfall.

In the twentieth century, Coumshingaun became the unlikely abode of yet another reclusive character, known locally as Lackendarra Jim. Raised at Lackendarra on the western slopes of the Comeraghs, Jim Fitzgerald volunteered for the British Army in 1914 and served in France and the Middle East. Severely shell-shocked and unable to work on his return from the Great War, he found peace by withdrawing to an improvised shelter in this hauntingly beautiful location. Scenery doesn't, of course, butter the parsnips and so once a week Jim would forsake his mountain eyrie to collect an army pension and do his shopping in the nearby village of Clonea Power. Residing in Coumshingaun for almost 40 years, he became something of a local celebrity, with visitors coming from a distance to climb up and visit this apparently genial man in his spectacular upland redoubt.

Onwards now, as the rocky scrambling on the arête becomes both easy and enjoyable. Eventually it gives way to pleasantly elevated walking above great gullies that dive precipitously to the brooding waters far below until one final steepening bars your route. This is the Becher's Brook of your walk with very unfortunate gravitational consequences a possibility from even a small slip. It is certainly a place to proceed with caution particularly in wet or icy conditions. Once above this hurdle, however, you are safely on the great vastness of the Comeragh Plateau and are now at liberty to choose your own horizon.

If you lack confidence in navigation, it is best simply to circumnavigate the coum, keeping the lake to your right. Do a full 360 degrees and you will eventually rejoin your original route up from Kilclooney. This will shorten the overall route by 5km, 1½ hours and 110m of ascent.

Otherwise, strike out bravely towards the great silence of the featureless plateau to reach the small cairn that marks point 792m, the highest top in the Comeraghs. Commonly this is referred to as Fauscoum, but on the OSi map Fauscoum actually denotes the lake-less corrie directly south of Coumshingaun – so confusion reigns. Whatever its proper title, one thing is certain: this is a grand place to tarry and banquet on superb views over the West Comeraghs, the Knockmealdown Mountains, the Waterford lowlands and the distant sparkle of the Atlantic Ocean.

Next go north-east to pick up the precipice west of Coumshingaun and follow its edge until it swings sharply east. Here you instead strike out almost due north for about 500m to reach a clifftop that offers a tantalising window on the tranquillity of Crotty's Lough laid out below. Tag the cliffs (right) to the prominent pinnacle known as Crotty's Rock which offers a marvellous vista and is the location where the outlaw is reputed to have kept watch for hostile forces. In such an eventuality, plan B was apparently a retreat to a claustrophobic cave located on the opposite side of the lake where all the advantages lay with a defender.

Betrayed by an accomplice, Crotty was hanged in Waterford in 1742 and then in a final melodramatic denouement his wife jumped to her death from the rocks where you now stand. Perhaps she might have been better advised to scramble instead through an aperture in the pinnacle behind, for legend holds that those who do so are guaranteed marriage within twelve months.

To return to Kilclooney, head directly south until you encounter Iske Sullas ('the water of light'). Keeping the stream to your right – but not too closely as there are sharp drops – descend until the slope eases below a final waterfall. Now traverse right to cross Iske Sullas and the moraines at the mouth of Coumshingaun. These will lead you to a path that ascends to the large boulder encountered earlier. From here it is a short ramble downhill to Kilclooney.

WALK 12:
The Circuit of Glenary

Option 1
Grade: 3
Time: 3 hours
Ascent: 240m
Distance: 11km

Option 2
Grade: 3
Time: 4½ hours
Ascent: 470m
Distance: 13.5km

Map: OSi *Discovery* Series sheet 74 and 75

Start & Finish: About 2km from Clonmel on the R671 Clonmel/Dungarvan road and just beyond a row of houses, take a minor road left. Continue uphill until Carey's Castle car park and picnic site are signed to your left. Your walk begins here.

Suitability: Generally an unchallenging outing ideal for those with average walking fitness although on the longer route some will find the pull up Lachtnafrankee a challenge. In mist, some navigation skills are required. Note: when water levels are high in the Glenary stream it is inadvisable to cross at Carey's Castle. Instead continue west to a public road and then a right turn leads to a bridge where you go straight ahead on a wide forest trail leading back to your parking place.

In the mountains south of Clonmel there exists a mock-Tudor mansion, a hillside farmhouse, an obtrusively unblended religious cross and a firing range. Now you may be wondering how the developers got away with such blatant intrusions on the mountain environment. The answer is simple: they didn't apply for planning permission. You see, most of the structures in Waterford's Glenary Valley are from a time when planning requirements were unheard of. The mansion is the eighteenth-century Carey's Castle and it was once actually due for demolition after falling into dangerous disrepair, but locals protested and so it was secured and preserved.

Walk 12: The Circuit of Glenary

Would Glenary be better if some forgotten planning law had maintained it, pristine and unaltered, by human hand? Probably not. Carey's Castle tells the story of a short-lived and misguided struggle to tame the uplands. And the deserted hillside farmhouse tells of a longer battle lost. Indeed, the drystone walls, the bridle paths and field systems of Glenary seem not so much incongruous intrusions as monuments to the endeavour of previous generations. For Glenary is actually a green museum to a departed era and for this reason alone it is well worth a visit.

To enjoy an outing that punches above its modest height in terms of variety and scenery, begin at Carey's Castle car park at **S186 191** (see panel above). Return immediately to the public road, go right and right again. Follow the Munster Way signs to the end of a minor road and then left and uphill on an increasingly muddy track. When open mountainside appears to the right, leave the track and head over rough ground to a stile over a wire fence. Now part from the walking arrows and ascend east until the going levels and an altar site and Holy Year cross appear ahead. Here there are superb views over Clonmel to Slievenamon and each year on the August bank holiday Monday, the faithful labour uphill in throngs for a celebration of Mass.

Next descend south-east on a broad track. On your right, you will pass the crumbling remains of a stone-built farmstead. Known as Park Grub, it was once the upland home of the Ireland family. Ironically, William Ireland, the head of the household, was in the early part of the twentieth century the only non-Irish person resident in Glenary. Born in Wales, he moved to Ireland and married a Longford woman before coming here to take up the position of gamekeeper for Lord Waterford of Curraghmore Estate.

Clonmel seen from the Holy Year cross.

He passed away prematurely in 1915 and it was almost inevitable that afterwards his wife and six children would lose the unequal struggle with the hillside. Inevitably, the forces of nature are now busy reclaiming their once-productive fields.

Reflecting, perhaps, on the tenacity of a wilderness area in recovering lost ground, continue uphill to the cairned summit of Long Hill and then veer south as the route drops to a coll. Located above a wooded amphitheatre known as the Punchbowl, this makes an ideal lunch stop.

If you would now prefer a longer outing this is the place to diverge – see details of alternative route below. Otherwise, leave the Punchbowl in a roughly westerly direction. The descent can a little tedious but soon you reach the valley and join a track above the busy Glenary River. Cross a tributary of this river – with some difficulty when water levels are high – and continue over a fence and into a wood where a narrow path rapidly leads to a forest roadway.

Across the river to your right there exists a field system and some overgrown ruins. This is all that remains of the once-flourishing village of Glenary, which in the nineteenth century had a population of over 200 and remained an Irish-speaking community into the twentieth century. Unable to maintain its population in more affluent times it was finally abandoned in the early 1960s. A genial man, named Tom Burke, became the last resident to leave, having lived all his life in the glen. In his later years he became well known for his Friday expeditions across the hills to Clonmel with the purpose of shopping and collecting the old-age pension.

Continuing generally west along the forest roadway, while keeping the river below and on the right, you will, by watching carefully, observe through the trees a ruined building on the opposite bank. Cross the Glenary stream at this point to visit the architectural corpse of the once-proud Carey's Castle. Built at the beginning of the nineteenth century on the site of an earlier monastery, it proved the ultimate folly of a newly prosperous school-owning family from Clonmel. Abandoned less than half a century later, it remains, particularly in evening twilight, a hauntingly atmospheric and strangely melancholic place.

Carey's Castle

From the castle a track leads an easy 500m through pleasant mixed woodland to the start point of the walk.

View towards the Ireland farmstead Glenary.

Option 2

Refreshed, you now tackle the 'kicker' of the day: a short but punchy incline that draws you upwards to the trig pillar adorning the summit of Lachtnafrankee (520m). The effort is worth it, for this is an exceptional viewing point offering a 360-degree vista of the Comeragh, Galtee and Knockmealdown Mountains.

Continue over Lachtnafrankee's south-west top (433m) and descend along a broad ridge to cross a fence at a point where an ancient trail, which once linked the now deserted village of Glendalough to Clonmel, bisects at right angles to your direction of travel. The route now gambols over a couple of unnamed tops while offering haunting views south over the Glendalough valley to the fertile Waterford countryside and Ireland's southern coastline. After encountering another fence, you pass the small cairn-embellished point 412, before descending to a gate beside a young forestry plantation. This is your cue to swing right.

Glenary on a frosty morning.

A rough track, beside a forest edge, will convey you downhill while offering a sweeping vista over Glenary. Eventually, a boggy trail goes right to the corner of a wood. Continue descending beside the trees and proceed through a gate to reach a forestry road soon after. By going left here, you rejoin the route you would have taken had you chosen the shorter option of descending directly from Lachtnafrankee. Follow this, as described above, to regain your start point, while being careful to take the right-hand option where the forest roadway divides.

WALK 13:
Knockanaffrin Ridge

Grade:	4
Time:	4 hours
Ascent:	500m
Distance:	11.5km
Map:	OSi *Discovery* Series sheet 75

Start & Finish: From Clonmel follow the R678 for Rathgormuck and Portlaw. About 2km beyond Harney's Cross, the main road swings sharply left but go straight ahead on a wide gravel track to reach a small parking place at **S285 180**. This marks the start of the Mohra Loop walk and here a map board outlines the route to Lough Mohra.

Suitability: Moderately challenging outing suitable for well-equipped walkers with reasonable fitness. In mist, navigation skills are required on the trackless section of the walk.

The Comeragh Mountains remind me just a little of a giant butterfly with the east wing formed by the great Comeragh Plateau and its surrounding necklace of steep cliffs and wonderfully glaciated coums. The west wing is fashioned by the unassuming hills above Glenary that offer a not hugely demanding circuit with plenty of interest along the way. Finally, the slender Knockanaffrin Ridge provides the delicate unifying spine of the Comeraghs. Appropriately this fine ridge also offers a five-star walking experience that is a foretaste of greater ruggedness to come on the memorable ridges of Ireland's south-west.

To explore the magnificent spine of the Comeraghs, park above Glenpatrick and beside the blocked-off entrance road to a ruined scout's hut (see panel above). Knockanaffrin now dominates the skyline and from this angle it comes across as one of our shapeliest natural beauties and may remind you of Croagh Patrick, which is surely Ireland's handsomest hill. Now follow the red arrows of the Lough Mohra Loop upwards by going right and then sharply right. When the walking arrows eventually

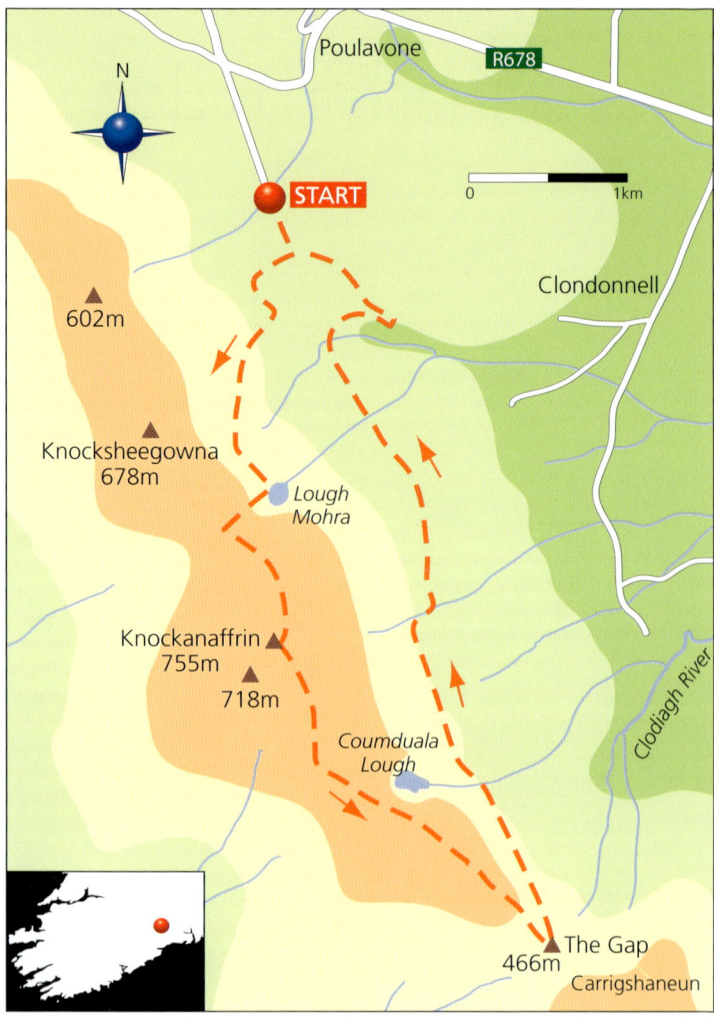

divide, take the option pointing straight ahead and marked Lough Mohra Spur Walk. Go left at a sign for Lough Mohra; cross a stile and follow a fence for about 300m to gain the lake.

Having paused to imbibe the blissful serenity here, you next walk up the slopes above Mohra on a short but steepish ascent to the ridge. You are now standing on the col between Knocksheegowna and Knockanaffrin on what is known locally as the Seven Sisters Ridge. On a clear day, you will now be enjoying great views over the captivating Nire Valley to the Waterford coastline beyond.

The slopes of the Knockanaffrin Ridge looking towards Knocksheegowna.

Next swing left and head up towards the 755m summit of Knockanaffrin ('the Mass mountain'), a symmetrical pyramid that comes with plenty of historic echoes from penal times when Mass was celebrated in remote places far removed from the prying eyes of officialdom. The ridge hereabouts is actually an unlikely place of worship since it consists of a series of rocky tors that now provide you with invigorating but easy scrambling opportunities until you reach the prominent boulder point that marks the high point of the ridge.

Eventually, a short descent accompanied by immense views into the jaws of the Nire coums brings you over a fence to a levelling of the ridge above Coumduala Lough. Those with silky scrambling skills can 'adrenalinise' the outing at this stage by descending an appealing gully to directly access this pretty tarn below, but those wishing to appreciate the ridge in its entirety should continue onwards through a marvellously unspoilt landscape to pick up a fence that canters straight downhill to the Comeragh Gap. Here white poles mark an ancient trade pathway that has now become a pleasant walkway, but this is not your route. Swing sharply left instead and begin contouring north-west beneath the crags of the Knockanaffrin Ridge.

You are now traversing trackless mountainside but the going should be pleasant enough as you continue below Coumduala and head towards a forest. The exact location point of the path you are seeking can be difficult to identify and so it is best to aim off by staying on a relatively high contour and then descend with a fence on your left until the forest track becomes plainly visible.

Cross a fence where a short, marshy track leads to a turning circle. From here tag a gravel track as it meanders pleasantly through forest and open countryside with great views over the Suir Valley to Slievenamon and beyond. Eventually, swing left at a T-junction and continue past a barrier to your parking place while reflecting, perhaps, that the Knockanaffrin Ridge is hard to beat for high scenic return for an outing requiring but modest endeavour.

Lough Mohra with Knockanaffrin rising above.

WALK 14:
Coum Larthar

Grade:	4
Time:	4½ hours
Ascent:	570m
Distance:	8km
Map:	OSi *Discovery* Series sheet 75

Start & Finish: From Clonmel follow the R678 for Rathgormuck to Clondonnell Crossroads at S312 183, which bears a sign for the Boolas and the Gap. Go right here and drive a further 3km going straight ahead through two intersections and eventually following a boreen to park in Curraheen farmyard.

Suitability: Challenging outing suitable for well-equipped walkers with fitness and some head for heights.

Problems with access rarely occur high in the Irish mountains; instead they are more likely to happen at upland access points. For a long time, the north side of the Comeragh Mountains was such an area. This fertile plateau came with access problems at Crotty's Lough and a pattern of intensive agriculture and small fields that, understandably, made entrance to the hills most problematic. And this was unfortunate, for one of the gems of the Comeragh Mountains is tucked away in this area.

Coum larthar – known locally as 'the Boolas' – is a compelling but little-visited corrie, mainly because, up to now, the principal route of access has been from the Nire Valley, which lies well to the west on the other side of the Comeragh Gap. Recession is, however, often the mother of ingenuity and during this turbulent period there was a greater emphasis placed on making the Irish countryside more accessible for tourists.

Fáilte Ireland developed a series of themed looped walks that can be completed in half a day or less, which return users conveniently to their starting point. One such trail in the Waterford countryside not only

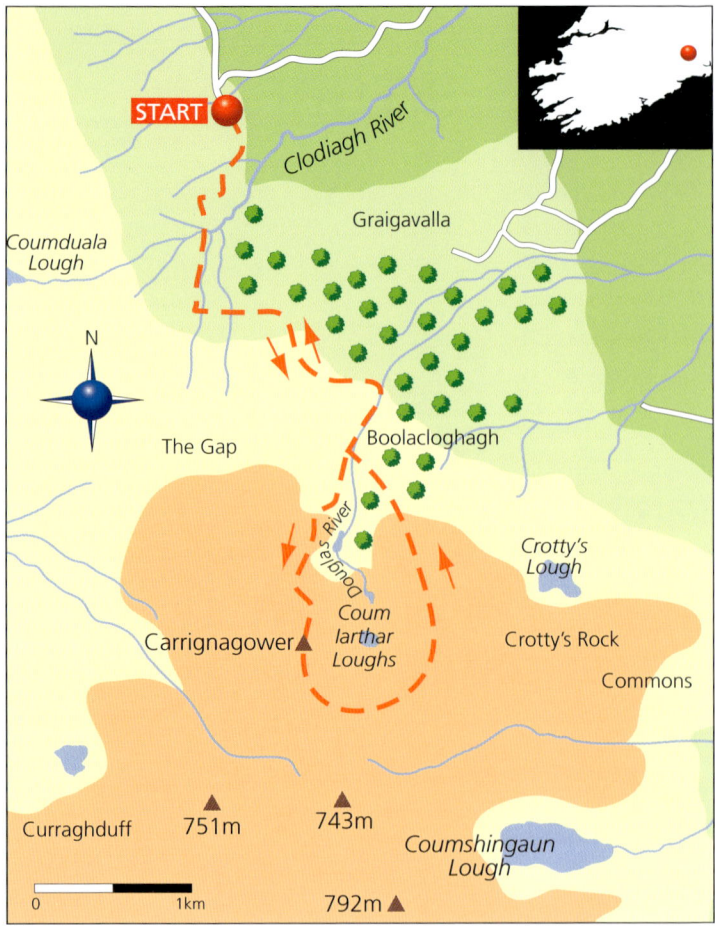

provides a lovely outing in itself but has also greatly improved access to the Boola lakes and the plateau above Coum Iarthar.

To explore the north side of the east Comeraghs, start from the Curraheen Trailhead, **S306 153**, which is located in an old farmyard built in the Irish vernacular style of having the farm outbuildings in a courtyard to the front of the farmhouse. Then follow the walking arrows along an enclosed rural lane before turning right and passing over a stile into a field. Continue following the arrows through a series of small fields and past a map board to reach open mountainside.

Here a spur walk is signed (right) for Coumduala Lough but you continue ahead with Crotty's Rock – known locally as 'the ass's ears'

Walk 14: Coum Iarthar

– protruding above the skyline as if a huge donkey were resting in the next valley. Cross several streams with convenient footbridges to reach the corner of Graigavalla forest. Keeping the trees on your left, pass a large rock on your right and continue to reach the infant Douglas River flowing at right angles to your route. Here, a line of white poles marks an ancient trade route across the Comeraghs. It is known locally as '*Bóithrín na Sochraide*' ('the little road of funerals') since it was used to carry coffins from the Upper Nire Valley for burial in Rathgormuck as there was no Catholic church in the Nire Valley until the middle of the nineteenth century.

The western cliffs of Coum Iarthar.

Scrambling towards the summit of the Boola Pinnacle.

Your objective, however, lies uphill. With the stream on your left, ascend into the impressive jaws of Coum Iarthar. Keep to the right-hand side of the coum and you will notice a great blade of rock that stands out from the cliff wall. Ascend steep ground now to reach a small grassy col directly inside this rock blade while admiring the wonderfully complex architecture of the coum wall immediately on your right. You may now notice that this rock pinnacle bears a distinct resemblance to Scotland's famous inaccessible pinnacle in the Cuillin Hills of Skye. About 100m long and 15m high, it is the only non-coastal Irish top I know that requires rock climbing of, at least, very difficult standard to ascend even by its easiest route.

Unless you are a confident rock climber, do not be lured into attempting an ascent of the pinnacle. Instead, this is a good place to settle and enjoy lunch, particularly on a sunny day.

Afterwards, continue by descending slightly and then swinging sharply right to scramble up a disrupted gully, followed by steep but more open ground to reach the Comeragh Plateau. From here it is possible to go directly ahead and soon encounter a fence that can be followed right all the way down to the head of the Comeragh Gap from where walking arrows will lead you all the way back to the Curraheen Trailhead. However, this can be an unpleasant, knee-jarring descent, where non-scramblers must be careful to bypass (on the left) a steep rocky down-climb.

A much better option is to go anticlockwise instead and circuit the corrie above its four picturesque paternoster lakes with the almost circular innermost Boola constituting the highest lake in the Comeraghs. Continue all the way around the coum and then descend on reasonably pleasant terrain to reach the floor of the coum beside the outermost lake. Now it is a question of retracing your steps by following the yellow arrows back to the Curraheen Trailhead.

Flowers bedeck a forest edge at Curraheen.

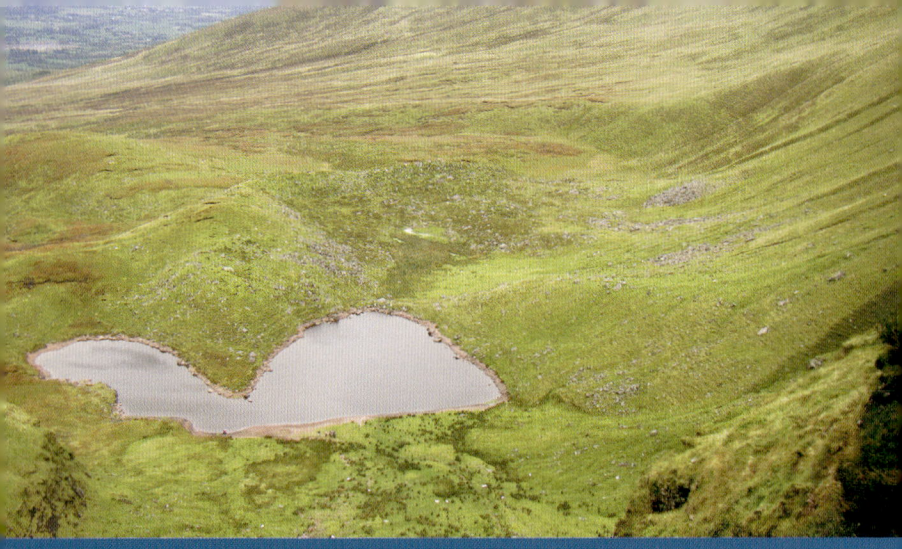

The unusual kidney-shaped inner lake at Muskry taken near O'Loughlin's Castle.

The Galtee Mountains

It is an evocative name for most Irish people, recalling mouth-watering images of sizzling fry-ups. The famous bacon brand has even managed to find a place in emigrant lore with Galtee products now a nostalgia-inducing gift to the Irish diaspora living abroad.

Initially, the eponymous mountain range may seem less appealing. From the M8 south of Cashel, the great rampart of the Galtee Mountains rises abruptly and seems to bar the way south implacably, with no chink in its mighty armour. Unlike the Knockmealdowns and Comeraghs, the Galtees consist of an unbroken rampart of great flat-topped peaks with no roads splitting the range. Indeed, Ireland's highest inland mountains formed an exasperating barrier to early railway engineers and forced the Dublin–Cork railway to loop into south Limerick and north Cork while the M8 motorway now bypasses to the east.

To explore these high mountains, it is necessary to forgo the world of motorised transport and gain height exclusively by muscle power. This is, however, facilitated by the fact that, for the most part, the Galtees are cloaked by benign blanket bog and present a reasonably undemanding aspect to the walker approaching from the south. The north side of the range is also easily accessible but startlingly different in character with a much more untamed grandeur. The jewels of the Galtees are secreted here – great steep-sided corries that chew into the mountainside to hold five austerely enchanting lakes beneath the shadow of the highly elevated Galty Ridge.

WALK 15:
The Circuit of Glencushnabinna

Grade:	4
Time:	5 hours
Ascent:	1,025m
Distance:	12.5km
Map:	OSi *Discovery* Series sheet 74

Start & Finish: From Lisvernane village, in Aherlow, go east along the R663 towards Bansha. After a kilometre turn right and then go left at a T-junction. A short distance beyond is Clydagh Bridge, and soon after the fingerpost for Galtymore points right. After about 300m, park at the forest entrance on the right.

Suitability: Be in no doubt that this is a challenging walk requiring good fitness and leading you to a considerable altitude. Be fully kitted out with spare clothing and raingear. Carry a map and compass and be aware that around Galtymore summit walkers become disorientated in mist with monotonous regularity.

It is sometimes said that work is the curse of the drinking classes. This may or may not be true but one thing is certain, employment commitments are a thorn in the side of those yearning the freedom of the hills. So many wonderful walks begging footfall and so few leave days to complete them! This tyranny of choice means that for most people it is a question of being selective with walks. If this applies to you and you can find time for only one outing in the Galtee Mountains, then it must be the circuit of Glencushnabinna. This high-level loop ticks all the right boxes as it passes over

The teardrop-shaped Borheen Lough.

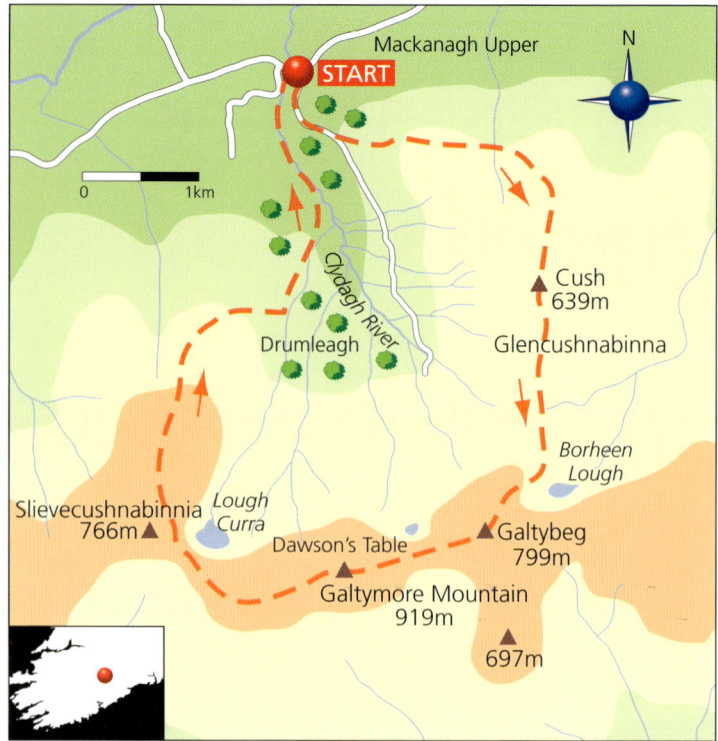

the elegant tops of three outstanding summits, including Galtymore where on a crystal-clear day Carrauntoohil and Lugnaquilla are at once in view.

For a great day on the hills park at Clydagh Bridge **R874 278** (see panel above). Then follow the minor road south into Glencushnabinna (spelt 'Glencoshnabinnia' on the OSi map) past another car park before climbing steps to a stile (left) and taking a path upwards. Initially the ascent toils through heathery fields before rising over open mountainside to Cush (639m), the first top of your circuit.

Marketing gurus generally hold that the three factors determining consumer demand are location, location and location. If so, this fine peak is simply in the wrong place to attract substantial footfall. For if Cush were transported to the Slieve Bloom or Cooley Mountains it would instantly become a renowned five-star ridge, raising its shoulders imperiously above the surrounding summits and acting as an irresistible honeypot for walkers.

Being a mere outlier to the higher Galtee peaks comes with the advantage, however, of remaining delightfully less visited. So, most likely

Walk 15: The Circuit of Glencushnabinna

Glencushnabinna, seen from the approach to Cush.

enjoying your own company, proceed along the wonderfully airy Cush Ridge.

Soon after, you descend to a scenic col, from where the next ascent is a two-stage thigh-burner. The effort proves worthwhile, however, when you sashay easily above the perfect teardrop shape of Borheen Lough before swinging right along the Galtybeg Ridge. And then comes your 'wow' moment: enormous views open suddenly south to the Knockmealdown and Comeragh Mountains while north you gaze over pastoral Aherlow to Slievenamuck and the Slievefelim Hills.

The short descent from Galtybeg leads to a col, made muddy by the growing popularity of the easier south route to Ireland's only inland 3,000ft peak. From here the ascent of Galtymore may not rate as a true thigh-burner, but it is a conversation killer, and you will doubtless be glad to reach the flat-topped summit (919m) knowing the day's hardest work is now behind.

Galtymore, viewed from above Lough Curra.

Here you are far less likely to find solitude, but your eyes will immediately be drawn to a white Celtic cross overlooking Aherlow, which was painstakingly erected by Tipperary man Ted Kavanagh in 1975. It is actually the fourth cross to be erected on the summit during the last century and its pristine condition is accounted for by local hillwalker and mountain rescuer Jimmy Barry, who for the past decade has taken upon himself the task of painting this cross annually.

Leaving the cross in your slipstream, head west along the summit plateau to a large cairn before descending towards an area of black bog where you pick up the Galty Wall. This impressive drystone structure was built in the late nineteenth century to divide the enormous landholdings of the Galtee Castle estate to the south and Massey/Dawson estate to the north. As a tribute to its builders, it still canters 3,500m along the Galty Ridge. Follow this wall as it traverses delicately above Lough Curra before parting company with it when it swings left.

Your route now continues generally north on a broad spur descending towards Glencushnabinna. Aim for a marker post on a raised knoll below and to your right, from where a line of poles leads to a stile entering Drumleagh Wood. Once in woodland just follow the meandering arrows for about 2km through sylvan surroundings as they lead you pleasantly back to your starting place.

Lough Curra.

WALK 16:
Lyracappul and Temple Hill

Grade:	4
Time:	5 hours
Ascent:	765m
Distance:	12km
Map:	OSi *Discovery* Series sheet 74

Start & Finish: Leave the M8 motorway at junction 12 and follow the signs for Kilbeheny. Go through the village and continue a short distance beyond, on the old N8. Turn left at a sign for King's Yard and Galtymore Climb. Follow this road straight uphill, ignoring further signs for King's Yard and Galtymore Climb, and continue straight ahead at a water-treatment works. Taking the right option at a Y-junction, continue to a four-way intersection where there are limited parking opportunities. Your walk now takes the uphill lane directly ahead.

Suitability: Although the going never gets terribly tough, this is a challenging walk that reaches considerable altitude, so be fully equipped for the high mountain environment. Carry a map and compass and be aware that the route, apart from the Galty Wall section, offers few navigational handrails.

Whenever I return to the west Galtees I immediately feel I have been away too long, for the outline of these insouciant hills immediately weaves a spell. The narrow pastoral valleys, drystone walls and rounded tops instantly recall, as they always have, strong resonances of the Lakeland dales and fells.

There was a time when I was a relentless cheerleader for these unfrequented uplands, but then I drifted away, seduced by sexier ranges with compelling gullies, rocky ridges and ice-crusted summits. But sooner or later I always return, for these hills beckon the rambler who wishes to leave the world of branded convenience and mechanised transport for the experience of true solitude in a timeless landscape.

Walk 16: Lyracappul and Temple Hill

To explore these little-frequented uplands, amble straight ahead up the lane from your parking place at **R869 197** (see panel above) towards the great whaleback of Monabrack Mountain. After following the laneway to its end, head out onto rough pastureland along a broad crest that leads just west of north.

The northern Blackrock Valley.

Eventually, the crest narrows and you reach the cairned summit of Monabrack Mountain (629m), which offers one of the most striking views at the heart of the Galtees. There are mountains in all directions from Galtymore to Temple Hill and Lyracappul to Knockaterriff.

So far so sublimely scenic, but now you are faced with an inconveniently steep loss of height to a col below the Galty Ridge. From here you have the option to follow downhill along a switchback track that was used to draw turf from the mountain in a less-affluent era.

The track leads into the Blackrock Valley and eventually back by way of the eastern slopes of Knockaterriff, but true mountaineers will be unable to resist the heart-thumping ascent that toils steeply up a spur to the Galty Wall. There they will find that this impressive drystone structure, built in the late nineteenth century to divide two great estates, is a most useful navigational aid if weather conditions are poor.

Whenever I encounter mountaintop structures such as the Galty Wall, I cannot help but wonder about the builders. Did they walk up each day from the valley, irrespective of weather? What kind of protective clothing did they have in harsh conditions? Did they ever get lost or have an accident on their descent? We will never know for sure, but one thing is certain, these teak-tough individuals created an enduring structure that, for over a century, has survived the harshest Galtee storms.

Magnificent views now unfold into the Glen of Aherlow as you follow the wall (left) to the tiny cairn at Lyracappul ('Confluence of the Horse'). This small eminence from the ridge improbably represents the highest mountain entirely in County Limerick and the second-highest point in the Galtees.

After Lyracappul your next objective is Temple Hill – the most westerly of the major mountains in the Galtee range. It is inadvisable to take the direct route, however. Instead, keep on the highest ground as you descend along a broad ridge towards Knockaterrifff Beg, being careful to stay above the great gullies that cut away right to the Glen of Aherlow far below.

Do not continue all the way to Knockaterrifff Beg summit but instead descend to a col and then ascend steeply to reach the shapely summit of Temple Hill, which is crowned by a great unexcavated burial cairn. These cairns are a feature of many Irish mountaintops and immense efforts were clearly made to mark the resting place of some now-forgotten personages, since such cairns are clearly designed to be visible from the surrounding lowlands.

This is your final major objective for the day and in clear conditions it is a place to tarry and enjoy the wonderful view across the fertile heartland of the Golden Vale to the distant shimmering outline of the Cork and Kerry hills beyond. Next, head downhill for a confluence of streams that marks the start of the Pigeonrock River valley.

Here is a serenely sheltered place to take lunch, as it is almost totally devoid of distant views and perfectly meets the requirement for oneness with nature. After your repast, leave with reluctance and ramble along the riverbank, as the valley grows wider. Eventually you will pass through double gates beside a new farm building near where the Pigeonrock and Blackrock streams coalesce to form the Behanagh River. This is where the shorter walk through the Blackrock Valley rejoins the main route.

Knockaterriff in the west Galtees.

For some unknown reason, no less a personage than the Elizabethan poet and Queen's favourite, Edmund Spenser, chanced this way and expressed himself enthralled by this meeting of waters. At the time he resided at Kilcolman Castle, County Cork, having obtained extensive lands from the Munster Plantation. His Irish excursion was, however, a short one: he was forced to flee to England when Kilcolman was destroyed during the course of the Nine Years' War.

Next you follow a roadway south with the Behanagh gurgling happily alongside.

At a place where forestry approaches the left side of the roadway, watch carefully for a blink-and-you-miss-it path, which represents the final sting in the tail of your outing. Follow this path steeply uphill, going to the right of an electricity pole and onwards to meet an ancient wall. You will notice the trees here are broadleaf and if you look through them you will see the reason why. They once sheltered what is now a ruined farmstead that offered a hypnotic panorama but has been subsumed by invading armies of coniferous forestry.

Go right here and continue over a wet section of path to reach a gate leading to the lane you ascended earlier. Turn right and soon afterwards you are back at your parking place. As you drive away, you will most likely vow not to be tardy with your next visit to the sublime west Galtees.

Pigeonrock Glen: looking south along the descent route which follows the left bank of the stream.

WALK 17:
Lough Muskry and Greenane

Grade:	4
Time:	4½ hours
Ascent:	635m
Distance:	12.5km
Map:	OSi *Discovery* Series sheet 74

Start & Finish: Take the N24 Waterford–Limerick road to Bansha village. Then follow signs for the Glen of Aherlow, but very soon take a left at a sign for Rossadrehid. At Rossadrehid, cross a main road to a minor road that eventually swings right. Park by an island of trees by a forest entrance.

Suitability: The walk into Lake Muskry follows a waymarked track all the way. There are a few steepish sections, and an out-and-back as far as the lake is suitable for family groups and strollers. If you venture on to the Galty Ridge, however, you should be well equipped and have the navigational skills required for high-altitude walking.

There was a time when you could spend an entire day traversing many of our best-known trails and not meet another soul. Recently, however, our trekking routes have become less neglected, with overseas walker numbers increasing rapidly and Irish people also recognising the breezy self-improvement that comes with outdoor exercising.

Of course, the number of trail users is not yet comparable to the Camino or Scotland's Highland Way, but there is still no doubt that the Irish countryside is increasingly becoming the playground of walkers.

So, if chance encounters are not your bag, you may now resign yourself to less solitary rambles such as the west Galtees and western Knockmealdowns. But if you believe that hikes are enriched by an occasional chat, the busy path to Lough Muskry is just the place for you.

To begin your walk, follow the indispensable walking arrows placed by the industrious Aherlow Fáilte Society that start at **R917 283** and lead up

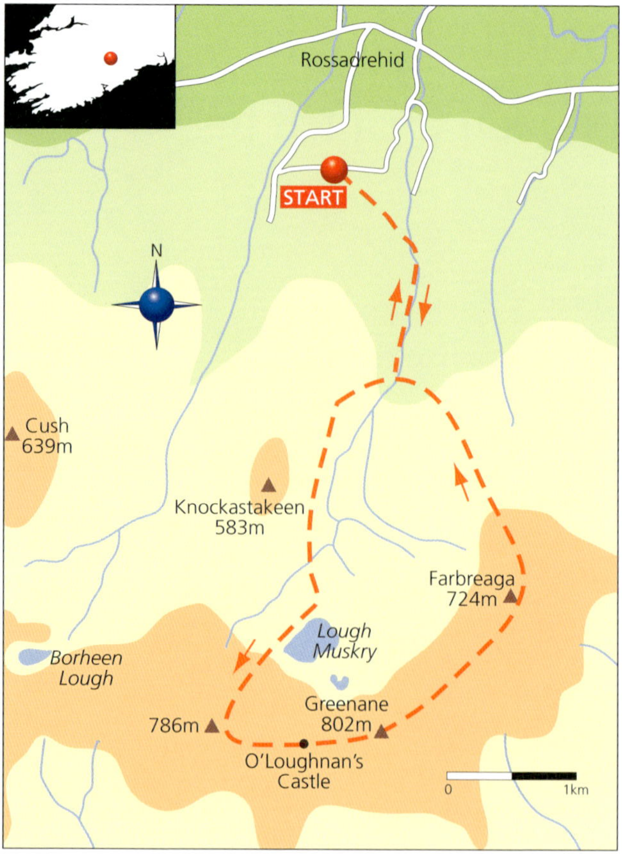

Lough Muskry valley.

Walk 17: Lough Muskry and Greenane

Walkers on the moraines above Lough Muskry.

through a forested area before trending right and more steeply uphill to a stile at a gate leading to open moorland.

From here the track, which was originally built to facilitate the extraction of water from Lough Muskry, roughens and steepens. In some ways, it is an intrusive scar on an otherwise pristine landscape, but it also provides a convenient handrail deep into the heart of the Galtees for casual ramblers and is, on balance, a good thing.

Now the moorland track undulates pleasantly, with the brooding gullies of the dark Muskry cliffs drawing ever closer. One more sharpish pull and you are beside the impressively large lake, which has an area of about 20 acres and a depth of over 100 feet. Local legend holds that it was once the abode of a slew of pretty damsels who, on alternate years, were transformed into birds.

It is almost obligatory for walkers to stop by the lakeside but eventually a decision must be made. If a short outing was your objective then simply retrace your steps from here and follow the walking arrows back to your start point. (This Grade 2 option will save 2 hours, 4.5km and 305m of ascent off the main route.)

If you wish to continue, however, you should now get upwardly mobile on the high moraines west of the lough and continue towards the slopes that rise invitingly to the right of the great cliffs and offer an easy gateway to the Galty Ridge. Head up the grassy slopes and then swing left towards the curious outcrop of O'Loughnan's Castle that sits astride the Galty Ridge proper. From a distance, this unusual edifice resembles a man-made construction, but it is actually a natural phenomenon created by frost-shattered rock dating from the time in the ice age when only the mountaintops protruded above the ice sheets. You will find, however, that today it offers memorable views past the Knockmealdown Mountains to the south coast.

Lough Farbreaga in snow.

Once you forsake the solitude of O'Loughnan's Castle keep the cliffs to your left while ascending Greenane (802m) and then continue north-east along the broad crest to a ruined building on the summit of Farbreaga that was probably a booley, which served as a shelter for farmers tending upland flocks.

Here the main Galty Ridge doglegs sharply right, but the route back to your start point goes roughly north-west and begins descending a sometimes-tedious spur that is, however, enlivened by views towards Galtymore and Galtybeg that show both mountains to their very best advantage.

Eventually, after crossing a stream as it enters a wood, which must be approached with great care when water levels are high, you continue uphill to reach the stile by a gate that earlier allowed access to the open mountainside. Now just retrace your steps following the convenient directional arrows to the walk start point.

WALK 18:
Galtymore from the Black Road

Grade:	4
Time:	3½ hours
Ascent:	610m
Distance:	9km
Map:	OSi *Discovery* Series sheet 74

Start & Finish: Leave the M8 Portlaoise–Cork motorway at junction 11 and take the old N8 south towards Mitchelstown. Near a derelict house just north of Skeheenarinky village, a fingerpost for 'Galtymore climb' points right to a minor road. Follow this for 3km to its end. Park in the small car park here.

Suitability: Challenging walk to a high summit that is often very windy and extremely cold so come equipped with proper clothing and footwear. Return from the end of the Black Road if unsure of the route. Have a map and compass and be aware that the second half of the route crosses open mountainside where it is easy to become disorientated in poor visibility.

It may not seem blindingly obvious as you approach for your maiden ascent, but this is the Irish mountain that resonates most with romantic associations. Cupid was hyperactive for well over half a century within the landmark London dancehall bearing the name of Ireland's highest inland mountain. Here, the god of passion spawned countless dalliances and an abundance of lifelong partnerships that sprouted within the walls of the Cricklewood venue. Until it finally closed in 2009, the Galtymore acted as a social club, home from home and gateway to romance for generations of Irish emigrants.

You are, of course, less likely to be pinged by Cupid's arrow on the slopes of the eponymous County Tipperary mountain – although stranger things have happened – but what you will certainly come upon is a fine, airy circuit with magnificent views as a reward for relatively modest investment of time and effort.

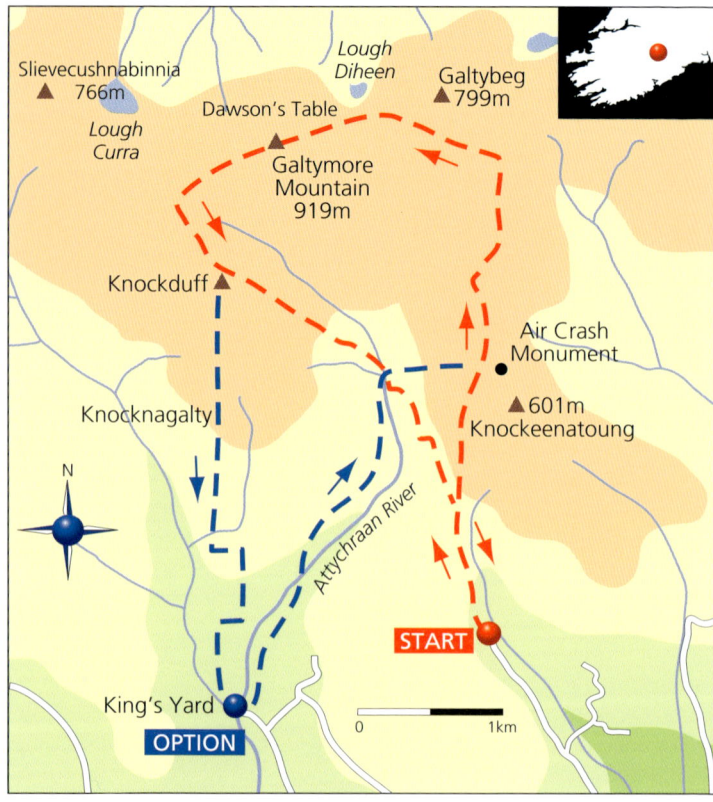

From your parking place at **R893 203** (see panel above), follow the laneway leading through two gates to a track on open mountainside. This is the Black Road, an old route previously used to draw turf from the mountain, but now a convenient high-level entry point to the heart of the Galtees.

After about twenty minutes of gentle ascent you will observe a stone monument in the shape of an aircraft tail about 50m to your right. It was erected to the memory of four Abbeyshrule airmen who died in a crash on a nearby mountainside in September 1976. This tragic event triggered the foundation, in 1977, of the South-Eastern Mountain Rescue Association, which now provides a comprehensive rescue service across several mountain ranges.

The going now steepens, and the Black Road swings right and then left before petering out in the shadow of Galtybeg Mountain. From this point head onto the lower slopes of Galtybeg, then swing left to reach the col with Galtymore.

Galtymore from Knockeenatoung.

Here countless footfalls over the years have rendered the peat hags muddy and unpleasant, but the compensation is a splendid view to the north over the renowned Glen of Aherlow and a more immediate vista into the unusual, vat-like Lough Diheen, lying 200m beneath your feet and reputed to be the home of a serpent. If you decide to linger in the hope of a photo-op, however, you should prepare for a long wait. Local legend holds that the shy serpent in the murky depths surfaces but once in seven years.

When the inveterate traveller Robert Lloyd Praeger came this way, he did not encounter the serpent but did remark on the 'savage grandeur' and lifeless gloom of Diheen. You may wish to reflect on the insightful accuracy of this observation as you now go left and (carefully) ascend above colossal cliffs to reach Galtymore's summit.

On reaching the top many people are surprised to discover that this is not exclusively a County Tipperary mountain and that they have also reached the highest point of County Limerick. Galtymore's twin-county, twin-cairned top consists of a somewhat concave plateau that is mostly cold, windy and inhospitable. The altitude and inland location mean that in winter it is regularly the realm of deep snow and it is not uncommon to encounter, during a cold snap, winter-sports enthusiasts tobogganing or snowboarding on the mountain's steep flanks.

The monument to the four men who died in the 1976 Galtee air crash.

Waterfall above Cooper's Wood.

Walk 18: Galtymore from the Black Road

Galtymore on a February morning.

Beyond the summit (919m), the plateau bears an iron Celtic cross overlooking Aherlow and offers perhaps the most expansive view in the south of Ireland. Not only is it possible to see the County Waterford coast and several nearby mountain ranges but also, on a day of perfect visibility, the view extends from the Wicklow Mountains in the east to the unmistakably slender outline of Carrauntoohil, in County Kerry.

Continue by first traversing Galtymore's west summit, and then descending in a westerly direction. Next, you should walk south-west across a plateau known as Dawson's Table, named after one Captain Dawson, whose estates covered almost the entire Glen of Aherlow during the nineteenth century. Then follow an expansive spur that descends roughly south-east without undue steepness to the confluence of two sprightly little streams above a forestry area known locally as Cooper's Wood, which lies at the head of the Attychraan River valley. Cross both and follow a well-defined track that initially skirts a wood but then strikes uphill across moorland to rejoin the Black Road about 400m beyond the previously encountered second gate. Now retrace your steps downhill to your parking place.

Option 2 (King's Yard)

Grade: 4
Time: 4 hours
Ascent: 700m
Distance: 10 km
Map: OSi *Discovery* Series sheet 74

Start point: Leave the M8 motorway at Junction 12 and follow the signs for Kilbeheny. Go through the village and turn left at a sign for Galtymore. Follow these signs to King's Yard.

If you think you might enjoy a slightly longer outing with the added benefit of secure parking, King's Yard R875 199 is the start point for you. Ideally located in a secluded little glade on the southern edge of the Galtees, this is where Bridget and Stephen Ryan have, as a fine example of rural diversification, offered café, camping, toilet and shower facilities to walkers, for over a decade.

Having paid the modest parking fee, head briefly south before going left and following the boomerang-shaped Cooper's Wood valley uphill. A serene path through mixed woodland above the soothing murmur of the rushing waters now offers you a handrail to a bridge across the Attychraan River. Just beyond, a rough track leads up a bank and over a fence to open mountain. With forestry now on your right, continue uphill until the trees finally peter out. Cross two sprightly streams before going east and up a punchy little ascent to gain the Black Road near the air-crash site.

Now follow the route as described in the main text until descending from Galtymore summit. Instead of swinging south-east towards Cooper's Wood, go directly south over Knockduff Mountain and then down to the high point of Galtycastle. With your destination now in view, continue by a faint path leading to a sheep pen. Here, a track doglegs easily downhill to deposit you back in King's Yard and the almost irresistible temptation of a coffee in the tiny farmyard café.

Looking from Knocknafallia summit plateau towards Knocknagnauv with Knockmealdown and Knockmoylan in the background.

The Knockmealdown Mountains

When Robert Lloyd Praeger encountered the Knockmealdown Mountains on his famous exploration of the Irish landscape, he was not overly impressed. 'There is nothing except this single row of summits – no lakes or corries, deep glens or cliffs; very little bare rock.' Quite apart from the fact that he was obviously incorrect – Bay Lough is a fine example of a corrie lake at the heart of the Knockmealdowns – he was probably also just a bit unfair.

Sure, the Knockmealdowns have been rather too generously planted with conifers, are overshadowed by the higher Galtees and lack the rugged grandeur of the Comeragh coums, but they should, nevertheless, not be ignored by the discerning hillwalker, for in every respect they form a proper mountain range. These tranquil highlands are also very accessible as they are bisected by three scenic roads through high mountain passes and also by the Glengalla stream valley, which divides the central Knockmealdowns but can only be traversed on foot.

A visit to the Knockmealdowns rewards the walker with well-defined peaks offering excellent viewpoints, some of the least-wet underfoot conditions in Ireland and an inescapable feeling of getting away from it all on less frequented summits that seem to encapsulate the true freedom of the hills.

WALK 19:
Mount Melleray Abbey and the Knockmealdown Ridge

Grade:	4
Time:	4½ hours
Ascent:	580m
Distance:	11.5km
Map:	OSi *Discovery* Series sheet 74

Start & Finish: From Cappoquin, County Waterford, follow the R669. At The Cats Bar, go right. The entrance to Mount Melleray is on the left.

Suitability: Demanding outing requiring reasonable fitness. Navigation skills are necessary, as the route follows high mountain terrain that is not waymarked.

Abbeys are islands of serenity in a troubled world that tend to be magnetically attractive, even to the non-devout. Certainly, the dreamy minarets of Mount Melleray Abbey, County Waterford, act as a lodestone that few travellers crossing the Vee Gap of the Knockmealdown Mountains can resist.

It was true that, for generations of children from the south midlands, mention of the word 'Vee' created an inevitable quickening of the pulse. In less-affluent times, when young people were still allowed to make playgrounds of the fields and woodlands of rural Ireland, crossing the Vee counted as a high adventure to the exotic coastal lands beyond the Knockmealdown Mountains. There lay the great Cistercian abbey of Mount Melleray and the promise of exploring its famous groves and enjoying 'meat tea' and currant cake from kindly but resolutely unspeaking monks.

These diligently prayerful monks rendered the unforgiving uplands productive in the centuries since the Cistercian Order returned to Ireland in their second coming, which followed their post-Reformation

Walk 19: Mount Melleray Abbey and the Knockmealdown Ridge

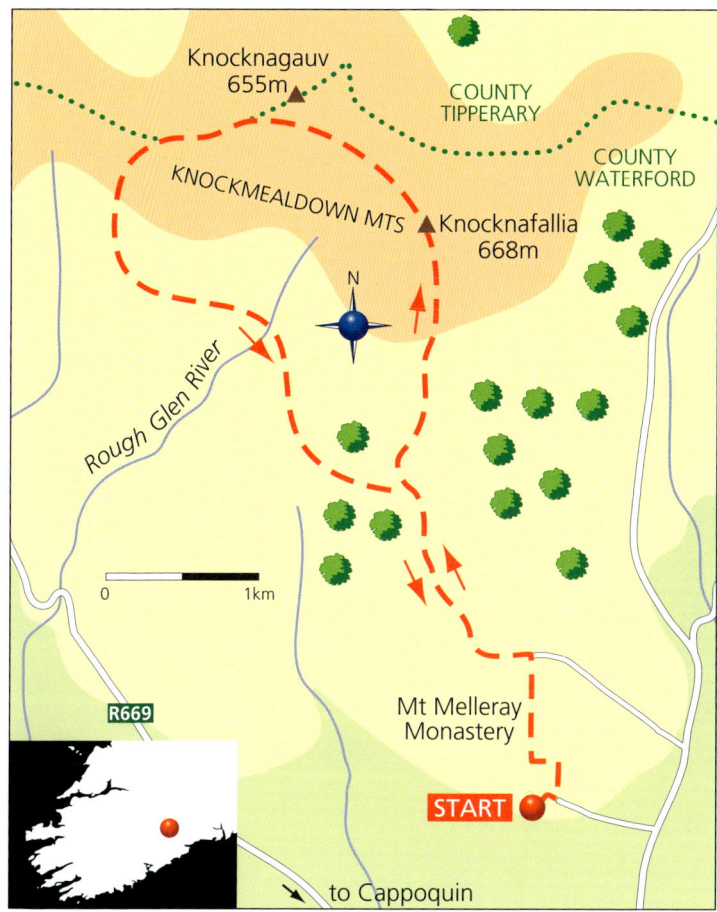

banishment. Working with the maxim that what is useful should also be beautiful they created some delightful buildings at Melleray, including the undoubted jewel in the crown, the abbey church. You don't have to be particularly religious to find this a special place and a trip inside provides an immediate sense of ageless tranquillity difficult to find elsewhere in the modern world. The monks' most renowned role was, however, as comfort to the many troubled souls who journeyed here seeking consolation in an era when the words 'counselling' and 'psychotherapy' had yet to enter the modern lexicon.

The prayerful atmosphere will already have been emphasised on your way to the abbey, for you will have passed a secluded Marian grotto where a couple of car parks have been added. These were built in 1985 to

The Melleray Abbey Resevoir.

accommodate the huge crowds that flocked to the area following reports of a series of apparitions. A number of local people reported that a statue of the Blessed Virgin in the grotto had moved and spoken directly to them.

So far so spiritual, but to explore the hills that provide a mystical backdrop to Melleray Abbey, **S096 039**, follow the signs through the monastery farmyard and then upwards through the splendid groves of Mount Melleray. Signs for a hilltop cross will then convey you past the reservoir, which once supplied the water that ingeniously generated power for the abbey.

Abandoning signs for the cross beside a derelict house, you swing left and continue upwards on a rough track. Left along a forest roadway then brings you to a junction where another left leads you to open mountainside. Now, a steep ascent leads to the summit plateau of Knocknafallia (668m), which is embellished with a burial mound and cairn.

View towards Knockmealdown Mountain.

A hypnotically attractive vista over the Waterford countryside now presents itself from Knocknafallia: a land of slow-flowing rivers, rich pastures and soft-focus colours. Having imbibed this exhilarating prospect you should now traverse north-west over Knocknafallia's broad plateau until you descend to an embankment that segues into a wall near Knocknagnauv summit (665m), which is surmounted by a rudimentary cairn. Your odyssey continues downwards to a col, to gain the ancient Rian Bó Phádraig ('furrow of Patrick's cow'), at the wonderfully titled Bottleneck Pass. Legend holds that the Rian takes its name from a huge bovine owned by St Patrick that charged up the mountain in pursuit of a stolen calf. In fact, it is most likely an early Christian trail linking royal Cashel with the major ecclesiastical centre at Ardmore.

Perhaps reflecting on the timeless nature of this ancient walkway, you now descend left on the Rian for about a kilometre before contouring left again to reach Rough Glen River where a couple of streams coalesce and the hurrying waters descend in attractive cascades. At a point marked by skeletal thorn bushes that have been stripped by countless winter storms, a tiny canal, laboriously dug by industrious Cistercian monks, draws water from the river while presenting the baffling illusion of flowing uphill. Known locally as 'The Source', it was built to provide Melleray with fresh water and acts as a reminder to us that, until the Industrial Revolution, most technological advances in Europe emerged from monasteries.

These days the main use for The Source is as a convenient navigational handrail for walkers crossing the uplands. Following it across open mountainside will take you to a stile and then along a rough track that leads to a solid forest roadway. Here, it's left and straight through a junction before descending right at the next intersection. Just before reaching a large turning circle, a stony path leads right and down to the ruined dwelling encountered earlier, from which you merely retrace your steps to the walk start point.

It is sometimes said that you are not rich until you possess something money can't buy. Melleray Abbey may now be on life support due to falling vocations but even in aggressively materialistic and secular times, its loss should be a cause, even to non-believers, for regret. It is good news then that, at the time of writing, there was a ray of hope for the abbey. A new abbot had been appointed and a large committee of well-wishers put in place with the objective of returning Mount Melleray to a sound financial footing and increasing vocations to the Cistercian order.

Your ramble finally ends beside the lovely cut-stone edifice of the renowned monastery, which is a good place to reflect on how generations of Cistercian monks have provided the multitudes coming to Mount Melleray with a retreat from the insanity of modern living while themselves cherishing the true richness of owning nothing.

Returning to Mount Melleray Abbey .

WALK 20:

Bay Lough, the Sugarloaf and Knockmoylan

Option 1	
Grade:	3/4
Time:	3 hours
Ascent:	480m
Distance:	7km

Option 2	
Grade:	4
Time:	4½ hours
Ascent:	860m
Distance:	11km

Map: OSi *Discovery* Series sheet 74

Start & Finish: Leave the M8 at junction 10 or 11 for Cahir. Take the R668 through Ballylooby and Clogheen. The walk begins from the parking place, which is on the right beside the first hairpin bend.

Suitability: A moderate challenge for walkers with a reasonable level of fitness. In mist, it would be better for those without navigational skills to return from the summit of the Sugarloaf to the R668 by the route of ascent, using the earthen bank as a guide.

At the head of the Vee Gap of the Knockmealdown Mountains, there exists a couple of unusual dome-shaped buildings. One is a shrine to the Virgin Mary and the other once acted as a staging post for the horse-drawn long cars of Charles Bianconi. A penniless Italian emigrant to Ireland, he rose, in the style of Ryanair's Michael O'Leary, to create Ireland's first budget transportation system. One of the country's first true experts in branding and using a low-cost model, Bianconi delivered inexpensive and punctual service. The Vee is certainly a good place to step back in history and visualise the nineteenth-century long cars and sweating horses of Charles Bianconi toiling upward past Bay Lough to the head of the gap.

The present, much higher, road across the Vee was begun as a famine-relief project in the 1840s. Today, it offers one of Ireland's outstanding scenic drives as it meanders between the Sugarloaf Mountain, standing imperiously above, and Bay Lough's lonesome curl of water. Hiking

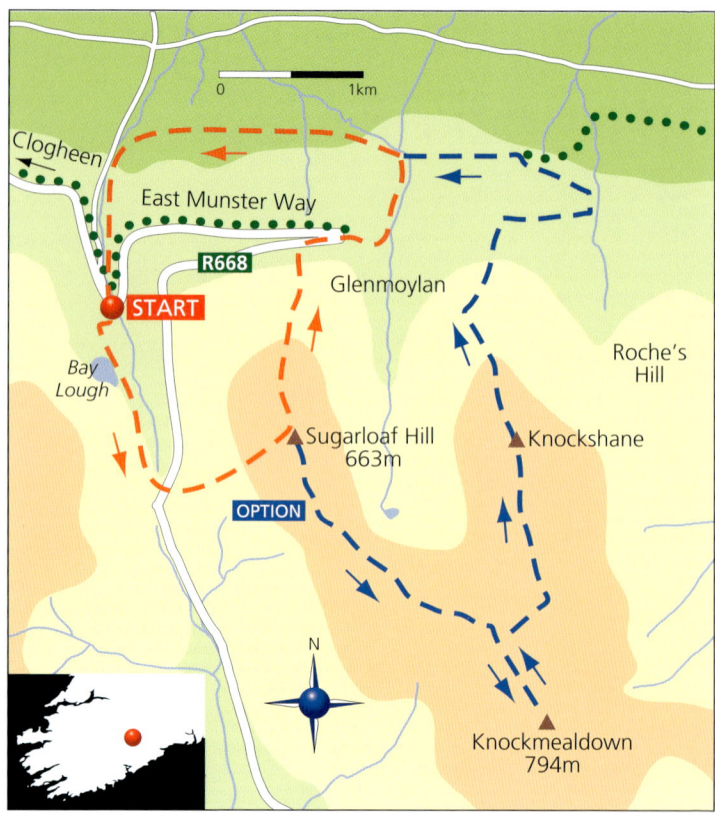

opportunities abound in an area renowned for its rich folklore and abundant historic resonances.

To explore the area, start from a parking place at **S027 113** (see panel above) and follow a stony track uphill through dense vegetation. In June, the area is a riot of pink-flowering rhododendron. Visitors observing the luxuriant spectacle are mostly unaware that this seemingly attractive shrub is actually a considerable woodland pest. It forms impenetrable thickets that now threaten the fragile ecosystems of many forest areas.

In about fifteen minutes you reach the point where glaciation has re-engineered the mountain to create brooding Bay Lough. It is unlikely that you will see bathers here, though, for a deeply held local tradition warns that the ghostly arm of a witch, Petticoat Loose, will rise from her resting place in the depths to ensnare those bold enough to enter these lonesome waters. Such tales do, of course, tend to bend historic facts to suit the requirements of the age. In reality, Petticoat Loose was a local

Walk 20: Bay Lough, the Sugarloaf and Knockmoylan

Bay Lough.

woman named Mary Hannigan, whose crime was, in all probability, not witchcraft, but that of daring to be different in less-enlightened times.

Go left along the lakeshore and continue upwards on a broad track following what was the original pre-Famine road to gain the highest point of the Gap. Now cross the road and follow an earthen bank marking the boundary between counties Tipperary and Waterford, which leads steeply uphill on the west flank of Sugarloaf Mountain. It is strenuous going for about 45 minutes until you ascend a final rise to encounter a rough drystone wall and head left for the south and highest summit of Sugarloaf (663m). Its English appellation marks this summit out from nearly all the other Knockmealdown peaks, which have names clearly rooted in Gaelic.

If you have developed a serious walking habit, however, and would prefer a longer outing, this is the place you deviate – see alternative route below. Whichever route you choose, however, your effort is presently well rewarded, for the Sugarloaf is embellished by twin stony summits that offer exquisite views across Tipperary's Golden Vale to the distant bulk of the Galtee Mountains.

Having imbibed fully of the vista, descend north from the northern summit by way of a rather indistinct track. You should now be heading towards the R668 at a point just left of a hairpin bend. Continue descending until a curious structure is encountered just above the road. This beehive-like edifice marks the last resting place of William Grubb, a landowner

The ridge between Sugarloaf and KnocKmealdown mountains.

from a distinguished Quaker family with extensive holdings in nearby Castlegrace who died in 1922. Tradition holds that the curious shape of his mausoleum was determined by the fact that Grubb insisted on being buried in an upright position, to keep a better eye on his property interests below.

From here descend to the road and follow the R668 for about 200m (right) to a hairpin bend. Leave the road at this bend and follow the directional arrows from a signpost marked 'Spur to the East Munster Way' along a stony track. After a short distance, the track divides and you take the left (downhill) option. The track now meanders downwards to join the Tipperary Heritage Way and the East Munster Way near an attractive footbridge. Do not cross this bridge but instead follow the signs for the Tipperary Heritage Way (as described in the alternative route below) all the way back to your start point.

Walk 20: Bay Lough, the Sugarloaf and Knockmoylan

The Grubb Monument

Rhododendron in full bloom near the Tipperary Heritage Way

Option 2

Once you encounter the drystone wall after your ascent from the Vee Gap do not go left along the Sugarloaf's summit, instead, swing right. From here there are few navigational difficulties as you continue along the broad crest beside the wall as it alternates with an earthen ditch and provides a perfect navigation handrail. After about an hour you will reach the summit of Knockmealdown Mountain – the highest point of the walk. This is marked by a trig pillar that offers a hypnotic prospect over the Blackwater Valley to the silvery outline of the Atlantic Ocean beyond.

Now, retrace your steps by ascending to the col immediately below Knockmealdown. Here, leave your original route and swing north-east towards Knockmoylan, which is shown as point 768 on the *Discovery* Series map and is marked by a pile of stones. Next, head down the broad, heathery Knockshane spur past another cairn. Then aim off, by keeping left of the spur as the descent steepens, and you will encounter a stony path skirting the edge of a forest.

Follow this path by going right and continue until, at the lowest point, a rough track goes left and descends to reach a broad turning circle. From here, follow a wide forest roadway as it first heads east, then roughly north-west and finally west. At a Y-junction take the right-hand (lower) option and very soon you will encounter signs for the Tipperary Heritage Way, which at this point has joined the East Munster Way.

Follow the walking arrow signs to the left across a footbridge and continue through heathery terrain to enter a forest and eventually part company with the East Munster Way. Continue by following the waymarkers for the Tipperary Heritage Way and finally you will emerge from the forest at the picturesque bridge beside your parking place.

WALK 21:
The High Knockmealdowns

Grade:	4
Time:	6½ hours
Ascent:	1,215m
Distance:	20km
Map:	OSi *Discovery* Series sheet 74.

Start & Finish: The village of Goatenbridge – shown inexplicably as 'Goat's Br' on the OSi map – is located about 5km west of Newcastle village, County Tipperary. From this tiny hamlet, containing just a shop and a large pub, follow a minor road south to a three-way junction, where there is an intersection with the East Munster Way. There is plenty of parking space here and this is the start point for your walk.

Suitability: A demanding walk requiring good levels of fitness. Competent route-finding skills are also required where the route departs from the navigational handrail of the Knockmealdown embankment.

If there is a mountain circuit in Ireland that could justifiably be described as knocking on heaven's door, the full circuit of the central Knockmealdowns must surely claim the distinction. The reason is not that this fine route straddling the border between Tipperary and Waterford possesses some of Ireland's most elevated uplands or highest peaks, for it does not. Instead, virtually every summit here comes with the initial moniker 'knock' attached.

Begin your walk at **S080 121** (see panel above) and follow the signs (left) for the East Munster Way and the Liam Lynch Monument. If any of the signs happen to be missing, the sequence to follow is: right at the first junction, left at the next and then left again before continuing straight ahead to reach the entrance to the Liam Lynch Monument. This is a 20m-high memorial in the form of a round tower erected in 1935 to the memory of Liam Lynch, the chief of staff of the anti-treaty forces during the Irish Civil War.

Walk 21: The High Knockmealdowns

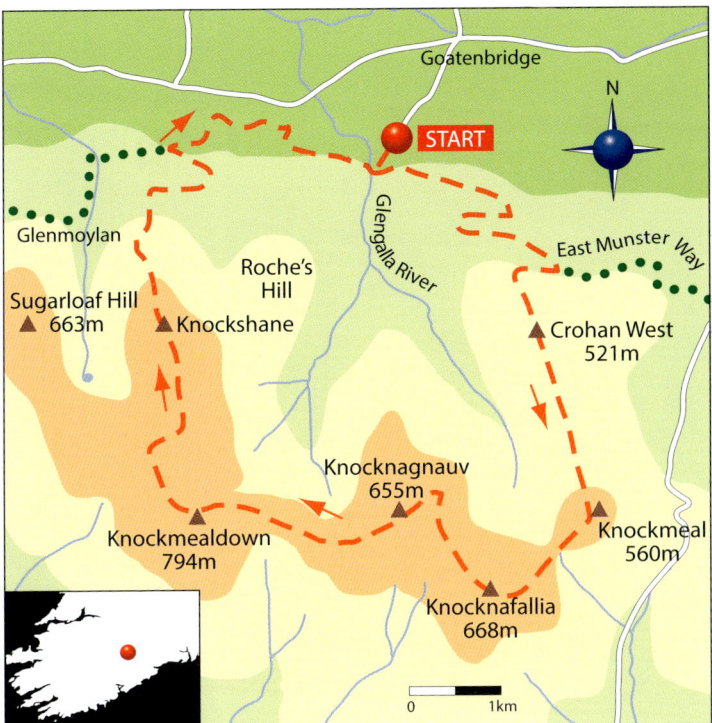

The sad events that took place here neatly encapsulate the huge tragedy that was this war. The monument marks the location where Lynch was wounded in a gun battle and then captured on 10 April 1923 by former comrades who were now members of the Free State Army. Despite the fact that he was a bitter and deadly opponent of those who accepted the treaty with Britain, the soldiers made every effort to save the badly wounded Lynch. Laboriously they carried their former comrade using an improvised stretcher on the long journey down the mountainside to Nugent's Pub in Newcastle village. From here he was transferred by ambulance to Clonmel Hospital where he succumbed to his wounds. Before passing away, however, he presented his captors with a gold pen as a poignant symbol of respect for the erstwhile companions he had served with in the War of Independence. And Ireland's strong consciousness of its history has ensured that Lynch has not been forgotten. Almost a century after his death, a large crowd still congregates here each year, on a July Sunday, for a Liam Lynch commemoration.

From the Lynch Monument follow a difficult-to-detect trail that runs roughly west from the monument and enters the forest. At the edge of the

The Liam Lynch Monument.

trees go left along a narrow track that leads to open mountainside. Now it is just a question of taking the track upwards as it follows a line of disused fence posts to reach the summit of Crohan West (521m). Since this summit is an outlier at the northern extremity of the Knockmealdowns there are grand views to the Comeraghs, Slievenamon and the Galtee Mountains.

Two low walls extend from Crohan West. Take the one on the left and follow it through often tedious underfoot conditions. The wall, and sometimes embankment, run more or less in a straight line on the west side of the ridge crest to Knockmeal (560m) where it is necessary to divert left more than 100m to visit the summit cairn.

Now rejoin the embankment, which denotes the boundary between Tipperary and Waterford, and descend easily to a col that marks the upper end of the Glengalla River valley. Here you have a choice to follow the embankment as it rises and then doglegs to reach the summit of Knocknagnauv. But this is to ignore Knocknafallia, which is one of the best viewpoints on the route. So, leave the security of the embankment and pursue a faint track straight ahead and sharply upwards to reach the summit plateau (668m). This is embellished by a widely separated prehistoric burial mound and a stone cairn.

Head to the burial mound – which has been disturbed to create a shelter – and enjoy outrageously photogenic views over the great meandering River Blackwater to the silvery outline of the southern ocean

The High Knockmealdowns from Crohan West.

beyond. Directly below is the rather dreamy outline of the renowned Cistercian abbey of Mount Melleray.

The original Melleray Abbey was located in Brittany until its monks were expelled from France in 1830. Taking advantage of new religious freedom in the nineteenth century, they came to Ireland under the leadership of Abbot Vincent Ryan. They briefly settled at Rathmore, County Kerry, before founding a new Mount Melleray among the foothills of the Knockmealdown Mountains.

Now traverse the flat summit plateau to the stone cairn and then descend to the col between Knocknafallia and Knocknagnauv to pick up the embankment once again and follow it until it becomes a stone wall near Knocknagnauv summit (665m). Your roller-coaster ride continues now as you descend to the next broad col that is bisected by the ancient Rian Bó Phádraig, an ancient trail linking royal Cashel with the major ecclesiastical centre at Ardmore.

Now follow the stiffest ascent of the day where you rise 240m to the summit of Knockmealdown Mountain (794m), the highest point in the eponymous range. The mountaintop is marked by a trig point and offers extensive views in all directions. Next descend north-west to a col where you part company with the comforting presence of the embankment/wall for the final time.

Instead you swing north-east and track the route as described in Walk 20 (Option 2) over Knockmoylan and down the Knockshane spur to reach the East Munster and Tipperary Heritage Ways eventually. Here, instead of following the signs left, swing right to trail the walking arrows eastwards along a well-surfaced forest roadway.

When you arrive at a large turning circle, the route scuttles left into the forest. You now pursue a much narrower trail passing over a stream by way of a simple log-pole bridge to emerge finally from the wood at a solid forest road where you turn right. Then just follow the walking arrows by taking the left option at each junction to eventually cross a well-constructed bridge over the Glengalla River and soon after reach the start of your walk.

Knocknagnav and Knockmealdown from Knocknafallia.

WALK 22:
The Western Knockmealdowns from Crow Hill Car Park

Grade: 3
Time: 4 hours
Ascent: 360m
Distance: 9km
Map: OSi *Discovery* Series sheet 74

Start & Finish: From the south Tipperary village of Clogheen take the R665 for Ballyporeen and then go left at a sign for Shanrahan Graveyard. Continue to the highest point of this road and park in Crow Hill car park.

Suitability: A moderate challenge for walkers with a reasonable level of fitness. The helpful arrows of the Blackwater Way and an extensive network of well-maintained fences aid but do not eliminate the need for navigation skills.

Are some of your fondest memories from carefree days when, in the style of Wordsworth, you 'wandered lonely as a cloud' through swathes of beguiling countryside? Certainly, this was true of famous English walker and guidebook writer Alfred W. Wainwright, who almost single-handedly popularised outdoor recreation in the north of England. A.W. so loved the solitude of the hills that he spoke on the BBC *Desert Island Discs* programme of dodging behind a rock when he encountered other ramblers.

If you believe Wordsworth and Wainwright had it right and that the uplands are best sampled in solitude, it may be that your ship has now sailed. Hillwalking has never been more popular in Ireland with the annual number of overseas visitors coming to ramble and hike in Ireland now counted in millions. The result is that finding true solitude on any of our

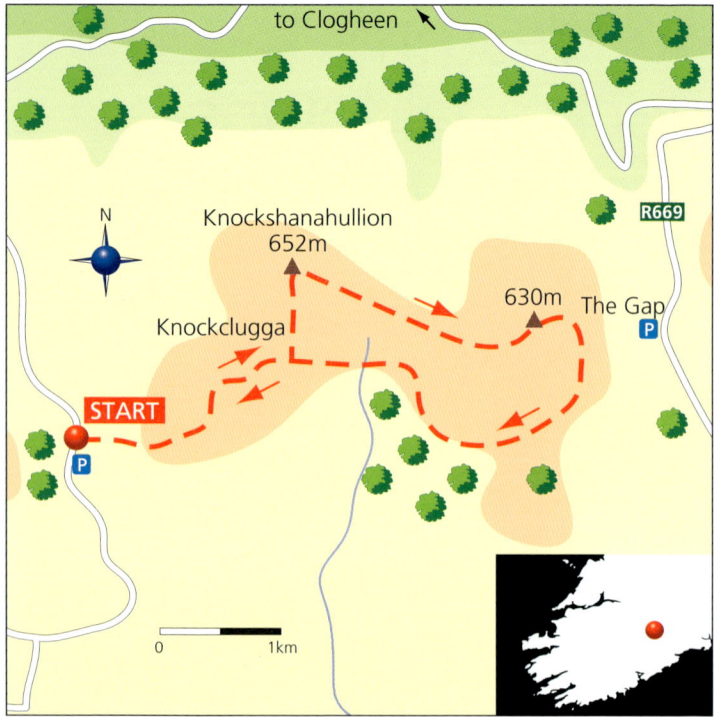

most popular trails is now increasingly problematic, but fortunately there are still plenty of refreshingly less-frequented landscapes where mostly you won't meet another soul. The gentle and generally dry underfoot hills of the western Knockmealdowns are one such example.

To explore the moorland landscape west of Bay Lough, set out from the car park at Crow Hill, **R982 090**, which is located at a walker-friendly elevation of 455m and represents the highest point of the western pass through the Knockmealdowns. After ambling north along the public road for a short distance, follow the waymarkers for the Blackwater Way east through magnificently empty terrain. Here, a stony path will convey you gently but idiosyncratically uphill for about 1.5km to reach the high point of Knockclugga, where a hypnotically attractive vista unfolds south over the Waterford countryside. Knockclugga isn't really a distinct hill but more a shoulder of Knochshanahullion. At a point, therefore, where the trail begins descending again, you must bid adieu to the marked route and head north along a broad ridge with gently rising ground to reach Knockshanahullion ('the hill of old holly'), which represents the highest point of the western Knockmealdowns.

Looking towards Knockmealdown Mountain from point 630m in the west Knockmealdowns.

The summit is topped the usual trig pillar and also by a large Bronze Age burial cairn. This has been considerably disrupted, but still serves what was, perhaps, its original purpose: whispering eloquently from the dawn of history about the beliefs of our ancient forebears. Further reward will come from the inspirational view across the Golden Vale to the Galtee peaks: flat-topped and angular to the west, gentle and rounded to the east.

Knockshanahullion also overlooks the once very prosperous village of Clogheen, which was, for a time, strategically located at the intersection of the main Cork–Dublin road and the Vee Gap into County Waterford. Just to the west of Clogheen lies Shanrahan Graveyard, last resting place of local parish priest Father Nicholas Sheehy. An activist in the cause of equal rights for Irish Catholics, he is regarded locally as a martyr, having been executed in 1766 on trumped-up charges of being an accessory to murder.

Leaving the summit of Knockshanahullion, descend south-east heading towards the corner of a fence. The fence initially leads east but when it swings south, you should strike out towards point 630m. The best advice is not to follow a direct route but to arc a little to the south so as to avoid losing height in the valley of the Glounliagh River. When you reach the summit, you will find it is crowned by a small cairn from where expansive views unfold east to Sugarloaf Mountain and the Knockmealdown Ridge.

Continuing east for a couple of hundred metres, you will encounter another fence leading south with a gradual descent to reach a three-fence intersection. Here you have the option – if you prefer a linear walk and have had the foresight to prearrange transport – of following the Blackwater Way east and downhill on a stony track to reach a forest edge. Go left and follow an undulating path beside the forest. Then begin descending a rough track, passing a shrine to Our Lady of Knock, before reaching the head of the Vee Gap. This option should save about 2km of distance, reduce the walk time by about 30 minutes and reduce the amount of ascent by about 90m.

If returning to Crow Hill car park, the way from the fence intersection is right along a trail that tags a forest edge. Taking the first right and later the right option at a three-way junction, you will rejoin the waymarkers for the Blackwater Way soon afterwards. Now, it's just a question of following the yellow walking arrows over a stile to gain open mountain and ascending a track to gain the Knockclugga shoulder. Then, it is easily downhill to your start point, while most likely not having encountered another soul all afternoon. As you drive happily away, you may just conclude that easy access to magnificently lonely summits is the unique selling point the western Knockmealdowns.

Looking south over the Vee Gap from Knockalougha.

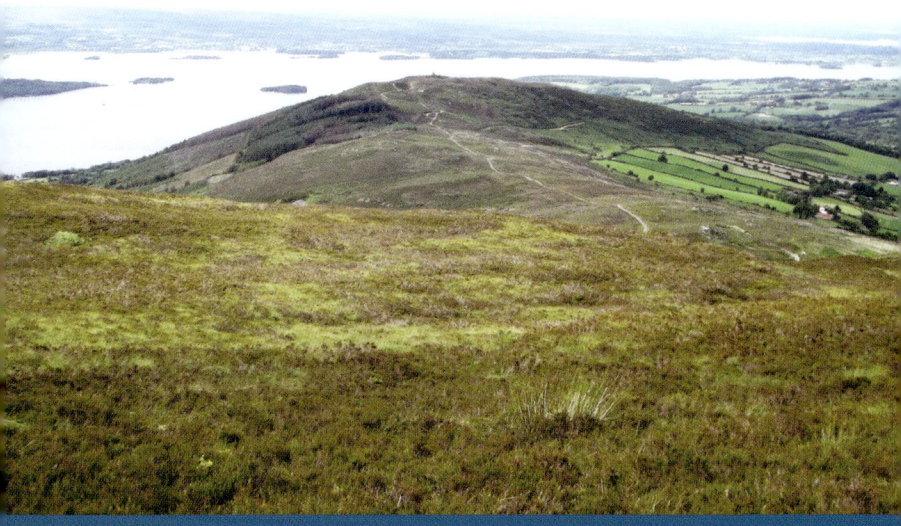

Looking from Tountinna over Laghtea Hill to Lough Derg.

The Arra Mountains

Mountains have always been special places. Down through the ages, succeeding generations have loaded them with legend and ascribed them with powers of spirituality and magic. It is the enigmatic quality of high places, their prominence and permanence against our transience and triviality, that draws us to them.

Nowhere is this truer than among the compact huddle of hills that lies west of Nenagh. Here people have lived and farmed close to the summits for countless generations with the result that evidence of human endeavour is everywhere. And the gentle Arra Mountains are still people-friendly, with benign slopes and the many criss-crossing trails footed by previous generations now bidding present-day walkers to come hither. A dense concentration of historic artefacts, mythological resonances and evidence of previous commercial exploitation then awaits to be uncovered by those who merely take the time to stop and stare.

WALK 23:
The Millennium Cross and Tountinna

Grade:	3
Time:	5 hours
Ascent:	350m
Distance:	16km
Map:	OSi *Discovery* Series sheet 59

Start & Finish: From Nenagh, follow the R494 through the village of Portroe to reach, on the right-hand side, the prominent viewing point and car park known as 'The Lookout', where there is ample parking. The walk begins from here.

Suitability: The route has one steep section but generally it presents few objective dangers or navigational difficulties. Nevertheless, walkers should have good footwear and carry warm clothing.

For a real sense of regressing in time, begin your Arra Mountains walk from a viewing point known locally as 'The Lookout' at **R734 810**. Located on the R494 between Ballina and Portroe, it offers an opportunity to savour memorable views over island-strewn Lough Derg.

From The Lookout, follow the waymarkers for the Lough Derg Way and the green arrows for the Arra Mountains a short distance towards Portroe before going right over a stile and on through bucolic fields and lanes to reach a road where the arrows point to the right for about 800m. Then it is left and upwards on a pleasant rustic lane. You meander through a disused slate quarry, which acts as a reminder that until relatively recently these hills were a commercial hub. Before the sun set on the natural slate industry in the last century, slate-quarrying employed up to 500 people in the area, with 15,000 tons of slate transported annually through Killaloe. Beyond, you cross a metal bridge and follow a steepish path where rudimentary steps have been added to convey you towards the summit of Laghtea Hill. Locally known as Cloneybrien, the summit bears the remains of a cross that was erected here to commemorate the huge outpouring of piety that

Walk 23: The Millennium Cross and Tountinna

surrounded the 1932 Eucharistic Congress in Dublin. It was subsequently destroyed by lightning in 1940 and was replaced in 2002 with the large metal Millennium Cross. There is now a stone monument on the summit recounting the names of those who built the original cross.

Descend by continuing to follow the Lough Derg Way for just over 1km on a path that is initially rough and steep but becomes more sympathetic at lower levels. On reaching a tarmac roadway, go right for about 500m to reach a large communications mast on the right where the waymarkers

Walkers approaching Laghtea summit.

point left and uphill. Here, a conclave of large stones forms a historical site that is commonly referred to as 'the Graves of the Leinstermen'. This moniker reputedly dates from Brian Boru's kingship of Munster when the hero of Clontarf supposedly showed himself as the ultimate tenth-century father-in-law from hell. His soldiers, according to legend, ambushed and massacred the King of Leinster and his entourage at this site as he travelled to request the hand of Brian's daughter in marriage. Myths, of course, tend to rearrange facts to mesh with later beliefs and, in reality, this site is of Bronze Age origin and, therefore, pre-dates Brian Boru by about 2,000 years.

Next comes sustained upward mobility along a wearisome zigzag path on Tountinna ('hill of the wave') – supposedly named after a biblical flood that, according to the ancient Book of Invasions, drowned all of the first Irish inhabitants. However, there was one survivor named Fionntán, who cannily took refuge high on Tountinna and thereby lived to recount the tale.

Tountinna (457m) is the highest point in the Arra Mountains. The summit experience is initially lessened, however, by the huge, ugly microlink repeater (or deflector) masts that dominate the skyline. Whenever I approach a summit such as Tountinna, I can't help reflecting on the fate of these masts when advancing technology eventually renders them obsolete. Will the summit be dismasted and the mountain returned to its former pristine state? Or will they be regarded as having become sufficiently integrated into the landscape to earn a preservation order as eye-grabbing monuments to cruder past technologies? I hope it's the

Walk 23: The Millennium Cross and Tountinna

The well-signposted but less-than-well-maintained Graves of the Leinstermen.

former, but whatever the answer it is for the present necessary to look past these intrusive artefacts to savour the summit vista. You will then be well compensated, for this mountaintop is a photographer's dream, with intoxicating views to the Clare hills across the opalescent waters of serene Lough Derg.

From the summit, continue following the Lough Derg Way until a small lake (Black Lough) appears to the right. Here you abandon the markers for the Lough Derg Way and follow the arrows left towards yet another pair of communications towers and then left again to tag a broad path skirting a forest. After a few hundred metres, cross a ditch on the right to enter woodland at a point where a pleasant, but sometimes wet, forestry path leads downhill. Follow this to a three-way junction. Go left here and continue along a forest roadway, with a pleasant little wooded glen on your right to reach another junction where again the left-hand option is taken. Continue descending along the forest roadway with disused slate quarries and an artificial lake now industrialising the horizon ahead until an asphalt public road is reached. Turn left and continue for a few hundred metres to reach a T–junction. Again, go left and somewhat uphill past several spoil heaps from the slate industry to reach the entrance to Killoran Slate Quarries.

At this point the tarmac gives way to an unpaved rustic path, known as Killoran Lane, which leads to another junction. Take the left-hand option here along a side road and, soon afterwards, go right where a sign says

'Millennium Cross 1,200m'. Now, it is simply a question of retracing your steps over Laghtea Hill and then following the Lough Derg Way back to your start point at The Lookout.

Author's note: The final descent from Laghtea summit may not be to everyone's liking. It is quite steep and, despite the addition of steps, it can also become quite slippery. Walking poles are a distinct advantage here but, in the absence of same, descend with care. Turn slightly sideways, take small steps and keep your weight directly over your leading foot in so far as possible.

If you wish to avoid this descent altogether, go right instead of left when emerging from Killoran Lane and continue along a minor public road to a T-junction. Go left here and left again at another junction. Soon afterwards, you can rejoin the route by going right over a stile.

View over Lough Derg from Tountinna.

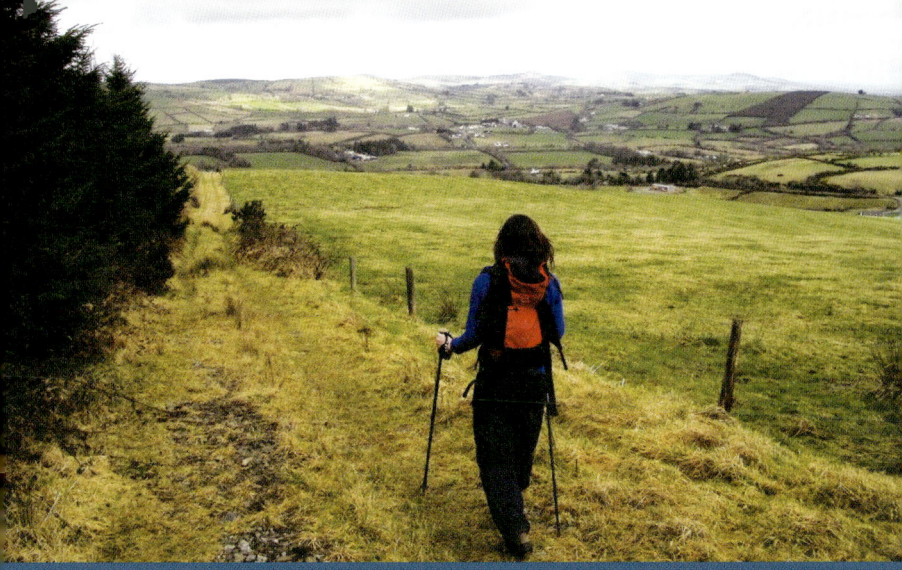

Walking the Knockalough Loop above Upperchurch.

Other County Tipperary Walks

It is sometimes said that all the best features of the Irish landscape are to be found in County Tipperary except for a coastline, although some would argue the shores of Lough Derg fulfil this requirement. Certainly, Tipperary is a county for startling and abrupt changes of outlook within an almost infinitely varied landscape. High mountains give way, with amazing suddenness, to meandering river valleys; woodlands march easily downhill to shake hands with expansive bogs, which then segue seamlessly into great arable lowlands such as the Golden Vale, the Suir Valley and the central plain of Ireland, which appear almost to groan under the weight of languidly fat herds of cattle These lowlands are further divided by a series of small but individualistic hills: the Slieveardagh, Slievenamon, Slievenamuck and the Devilsbit. Each one has, in some special way, become an important part of local consciousness with its own unique story to tell from past times.

WALK 24:
Knockanroe and Silvermines Ridge

Grade:	3
Time:	3 hours
Ascent:	255m
Distance:	7km
Map:	OSI *Discovery* Series sheet 59

Start & Finish: From Nenagh, take the R500 to Silvermines village, which is situated at the intersection with the R499. Continue south through the village for about 2.5km to gain the trailhead, where there is ample space for parking.

Suitability: In general, the route presents few navigational difficulties or other hazards. Walkers who opt to explore the ridge need boots and warm clothing. Walking poles are an advantage here.

The automobile has much to answer for. It pollutes our atmosphere, chokes our cities, isolates people from communities, contributes to obesity and exterminates us in thousands. Imprisoned behind glass, we are confined to desultory waves at our mostly unknown neighbours, yet we remain besotted with cars. Our love is obsessive because the auto brings unparalleled freedom: to go where we want, when we want, as often as we want. The explosion in hillwalking as a recreational pastime over the last century is mainly the child of the car; we can now visit sublime, albeit out-of-the-way, places past generations could never have aspired to, like Silvermines Ridge

Nestling beneath a camelback ridge, Silvermines village takes its name from a long-standing mining tradition in the area. Lead, zinc, copper and silver have been extracted since medieval times and mining continued sporadically up to the last century, despite the slaughter of more than twenty overseas miners during the sectarian conflicts that engulfed all of Ireland during the mid-sixteenth century. At its peak, mining employed

Walk 24: Knockanroe and Silvermines Ridge

many hundreds in the brutally hard and unforgivingly dangerous business of nineteenth-century ore extraction. Although coinciding with a fallow period for mining activity, with the nearby Shallee mine having ceased operations, the worst effects of Irish Potato Famine were ameliorated to some extent in the area. While multitudes starved across Ireland the families of those working at Silvermines were unlikely to suffer starvation as they were paid for their labour in corn.

For a bird's-eye view of the now-abandoned mine workings, begin your walk from the high point of Knockanroe Wood, **R845 693**, a place

View north from Knockanroe.

which is referred to locally as the Step. This car park high above the village allows you to reach a 390m altitude without effort. Follow the blue walking arrows for the Knockanroe Loop through a forestry barrier while noting that the first stage of the loop overlaps with the long-distance Slieve Felim Way. After about 200m, go left and descend gently through woodland to gain an expansive prospect over the lush and isolated Mulkear River valley. Here, you might reflect that if there were ever to be a contest for the title 'Hidden Valley of County Tipperary', this secluded glen would surely be in pole position. Standing sentinel above is the vertiginous bulk of Keeper Hill, the highest mountain in north Tipperary.

Having parted company with the Slieve Felim Way, you began ascending again towards the spine of the ridge. After climbing along a forestry road for a time, the terrain segues to a track as the loop enters trees and ascends past a couple of large boulders. Continue upwards through forestry to exit at two wooden pillars, where the east–west summit ridge intersects the loop. Here, the vista is in sharp contrast to that over the Mulkear Valley with the flat, fertile and well-populated plains of north Tipperary misting to a distant horizon.

For an agreeably short outing, it is possible to follow the walking arrows right at this point and return to your start point, having enjoyed a

Walk 24: Knockanroe and Silvermines Ridge

The Silvermines ridge.

Abandoned mine at Ballygown, viewed from the Silvermines ridge.

nice, scenic ramble of about two hours. But this would be to miss out upon a visit to one of County Tipperary's finest viewpoints.

Instead, you should strike out bravely over a fence and along the crest of the camelback ridge, which is defined by a path running west with reasonably pleasant underfoot conditions. Crossing a spot height at 470m, descend and then re-ascend to gain the highest point (489m) of the Silvermine Mountains. A great panorama now explodes north and west: the great liquid expanse of Lough Derg, the Arra Mountains of Tipperary, the east Clare hills and in the far distance the unmistakably angular mountains of Kerry.

Representation of a miner, Silvermines.

Directly below, your eyes will be drawn to the abandoned workings and tailing ponds of the main mining area at Garryard West. Immediately apparent will be the some oddly attractive stone buildings that are now bereft of purpose. Reminiscent somewhat of a medieval tower house, these have now been secured by a preservation order for they once housed the cutting-edge technology of the nineteenth century: the great Cornish steam engines that pumped water and raised ore in the mineshafts. Gazing upon the other scattering of now-forlorn buildings is a reminder that mining is a fickle endeavour, hugely dependent on price. In the end, it was a fall in worldwide demand that abruptly ended the mining tradition of the Silvermines in the latter part of the twentieth century.

The good news is, however, that at the time of writing, plans are well advanced for the development of a hydroelectric scheme at the abandoned Ballygown site. So we are, perhaps, about to witness yet another chapter in the long, industrialised history of the Silvermines area.

If you observe closely you will also notice how the timeless forces of nature are already busy rewilding the spoil heaps that stand as monuments to this once highly industrialised landscape. Reflecting on how the natural world ultimately defeats all human endeavour, you now retrace your steps to cross the fence encountered earlier. Here, a well-constructed path will convey you on the brief, but steep, ascent to the summit of Coolyhomey Hill, where yet another memorable vista unfolds north-east to the Slieve Bloom Mountains and directly ahead to the Devilsbit range. Afterwards, it is just a question of following the walking arrows on sympathetic gravel tracks to the serenely elevated parking place at the Step.

WALK 25:
Slievenamon and Killusty Cross

Grade:	3
Time:	4½ hours
Ascent:	530m
Distance:	13km
Map:	OSi *Discovery* Series sheets 67 and 75

Start & Finish: Heading from Clonmel to Kilkenny on the N76, branch left for Ballypatrick after about 12km. Turn right and go through Kilcash, following signs for Slievenamon summit, until the entrance to a stony lane is reached where there is plenty of roadside parking.

Suitability: The ascent/descent by Kilcash track is suitable if you are of only moderate fitness. On the extended circuit, the terrain crosses featureless upland with sometimes disagreeable heather so you need to be averagely fit. Navigation skills are also required on a misty day.

Once upon a time the ballad 'Slievenamon' routinely reverberated around Croke Park stadium on the first Sunday of September, compliments of the Artane Boys' Band. Those were the days when Doyle-Maher-Stakelum-powered Tipperary teams claimed All-Ireland hurling success with monotonous regularity.

Things have moved on. Premier county stickmen have found it exasperatingly difficult to consistently reclaim former glories, the All-Ireland Hurling final is to be contested in August now and we have the (more PC) Artane Band. Slievenamon remains as a constant, however, with the Charles Kickham-penned ballad still laying undisputed claim to the title of quintessential Tipperary song. An ode to passion unrequited because of separation, the plaintive lyrics 'Alone, all alone' are still guaranteed a sentimental rendition wherever Tipp folk mingle around the globe.

Alone in song and alone by location, Slievemamon is the place where County Tipperary secretes its soul and is an ever-present and unmistakable backdrop to the landscape at the southern end of the county. With

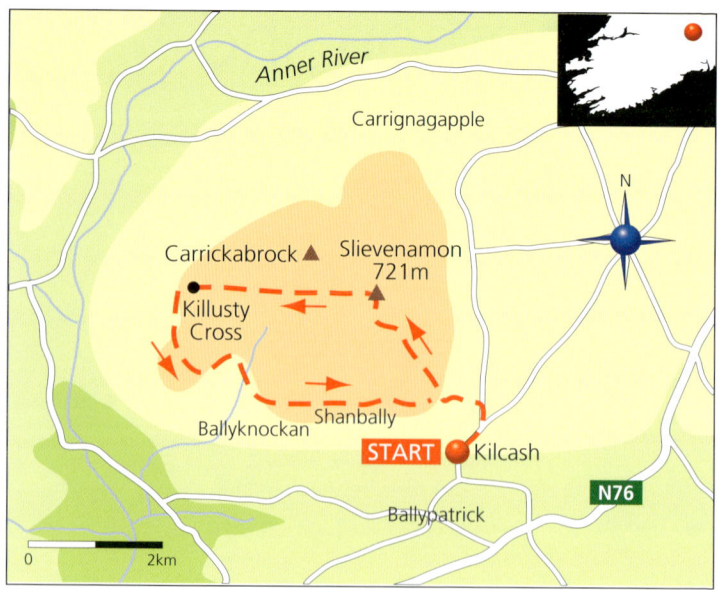

View over the Grangemockler plateau towards Carrigmaclear Hill.

Walk 25: Slievenamon and Killusty Cross

Kilcash Castle.

sensuously feminine shoulders that curve gently to a much-visited summit, this solitary peak provides much to justify its ancient title as the 'Mountain of Women'.

To ascend Slievenamon, follow a stony lane located above Kilcash (see panel above) which starts at **S317 288**. You will soon pass through two gates to open mountainside. Swing immediately right here past a simple cross, erected to commemorate a pilgrimage to the mountain's summit that took place to mark the year 2000.

Now an obvious stony track, which initially runs parallel to a forest, trundles upwards over a low rise and then heads directly for the summit. The going is never difficult but is somewhat demanding on the lungs. Halfway up you will probably be glad to turn around to catch your breath and gaze upon the vista of the castellated Suir Valley lying below, with the Comeragh Mountains beyond. Directly beneath, your eyes will be drawn to the ruins of Kilcash Castle, once a great stronghold of the Butlers. An unknown muse recorded the fall of this great house around 1650 with a poem that features the well-known opening lines *'Cad a dhéanfaimid feasta gan adhmad?*' ('What will we do now for timber?') It is still recited by local schoolchildren as a poignant lament for the decline of Gaelic Ireland, and you might while away the time on the last leg of your ascent by trying to recall the remaining words.

Surprisingly for such a salient peak there is no cross crowning the summit (721m) but as compensation there is huge burial cairn, reputed to contain the entrance to the Celtic underworld. A depression in the rocks is believed to be Fionn MacCumhail's seat, from which he watched candidates for his hand in marriage race to the summit. Legend has it that he cheated and helped his favourite, Gráinne, to win. Apparently, she was unimpressed by such chivalry. During the subsequent wedding banquet she eloped with Diarmuid, thereby creating the material for the tragic melodrama of Diarmuid and Gráinne.

Slievenamon has a flattened top, and so to appreciate the full view it is necessary to circle the summit plateau. Do this on a clear day and the tableaux of east Munster and south Leinster appear beneath. On all sides, fertile plains haze away to distant ranges. North and east are the Blackstairs, the Slieve Blooms and Slievefelim Hills. West and south are the Galtee, Knockmealdown and Comeragh Mountains to complete the upland necklace.

Killusty Cross.

At this stage, you may return by the route of your ascent (a walk that is shorter by 2½ hours and 7km than the main route described). If you are inclined to exercise further, strike out across the heathery mountainside in a westerly direction. At first you descend quite rapidly, then the moorland terrain levels out and soon rises gently again.

After about 2.5km Killusty Cross, which was erected for the 1950 Holy Year when there was a rash of cross building on the Irish uplands, will appear directly ahead. At the cross, you will enjoy extensive views over the Suir Valley and Clonmel. Beyond, the peaks of the Knockmealdown and Galtee Mountains stand shoulder-to-shoulder in a great semicircle. Next, move west on a track that descends from the cross to reach a forest. Go left here and continue on an undulating stony track that eventually crosses a stream as it progresses by skirting the forest on your right.

The track traverses a small ravine and then continues to a point where the forest edge swings sharply right. Abandon the forest at this stage and strike directly ahead on a track that traverses open mountainside with forest now well below you. Continue over a stream to reach the corner of a drystone wall and a junction with another track coming from the right. From here it is plain sailing along an agreeable trail to the commemorative cross encountered earlier and then down the stony lane to your parking place.

WALK 26:
Aherlow, Slievenamuck and the Jubilee 2000 Memorial

Grade:	2
Time:	3½ hours
Ascent:	170m
Distance:	13km
Map:	OSi *Discovery* Series sheet 66

Start & Finish: From Tipperary town take the R664 for Aherlow. Soon after negotiating a couple of hairpin bends, you will find the entrance to Aherlow House Hotel signposted to the right.

Suitability: The walk offers little in terms of objective dangers and should present few navigational difficulties.

The hidden Ireland of John Hinde postcards, so popular with generations of tourists, has been reduced by Ireland's recently acquired affluence to a mouldy metaphor for a supposedly simpler, happier age. And in many ways, this is a good thing, for only green-trousered tourists and urbanised Irish people, safely removed from the back-breaking reality of subsistence farming, still long for the nostalgic landscapes of a mythical Ireland. The supposedly idyllic lifestyle of thatched homes, ass-and-cart agriculture, road-roaming sheep flocks and farm families eking a precarious living from the land was terminated long ago by the EU, the JCB and the Celtic Tiger. These days, the Irish countryside is a place of pristine houses, productive farms and expanded villages. And amid such rapid change there are, of course, many egregious examples where we have been irresponsible with concrete blocks, created ugly ribbon developments and irreversibly reduced the quality of the environment. Search carefully, however, and you will find places removed

Walk 26: Aherlow, Slievenamuck and the Jubilee 2000 Memorial

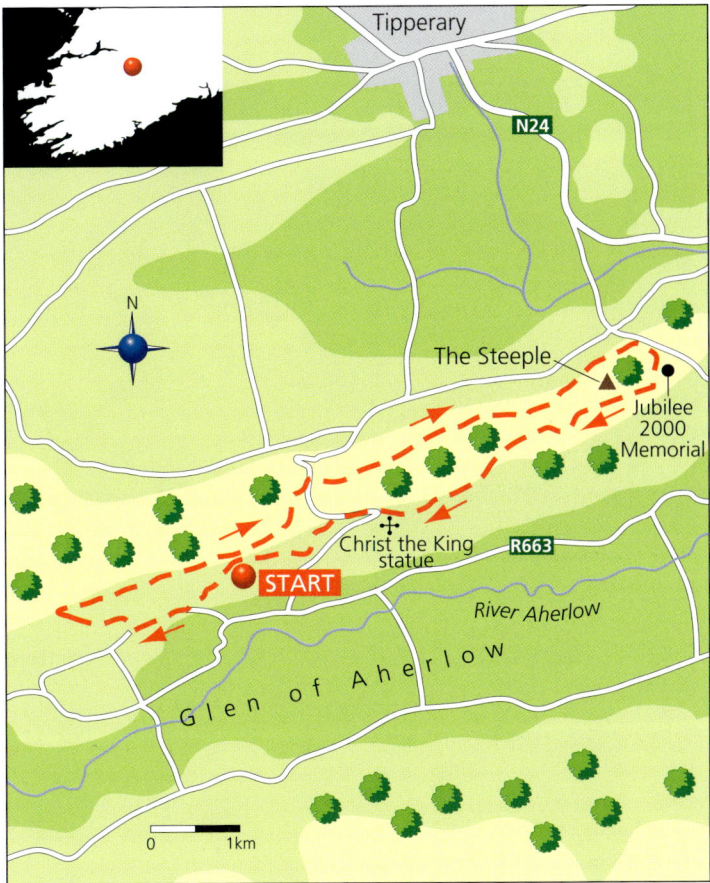

from urban hubs and tourism honey pots where life still moves at a slower, gentler pace, buildings relax easily into the backdrop and the lure of the landscape remains undiminished.

West Tipperary has such a place: a secluded glen that has resolutely defended its charm against the worst excesses of a globalised world. And above the Glen of Aherlow, the sylvan Slievenamuck Ridge offers an easy but memorable walk that is well suited for families and proffers breathtaking views to the Galtee Mountains.

Start your walk from the car park of the Aherlow House Hotel **R870 304** (see panel above), which was originally built for the Massey/Dawson family by the Irish government in compensation for the destruction of their great house at Ballinacourty during the Irish Civil War. First to capture your curiosity here is likely to be the Aherlow Ogham Stone, which is

Walkers enjoying a ramble in the woodlands of Slievenamuck.

located close to the hotel entrance and bears a fine example of the earliest Celtic writing.

Having satisfied your curiosity you then follow the tarred surface downhill to reach a sharp left bend where you turn right and enter forestry again. Now follow the purple arrows for the Ballinacourty Loop along a forestry track before swinging right and ascending through Ballinacourty Woods. After about twenty minutes you reach a T-junction where the Ballyhoura Way disappears left but your route lies to the right while still following the purple arrows. Here your walk tags the southern slopes of Slievenamuck Mountain, which is named after a fearsome sow that is reputed to have been put to the spear by no less an individual than Fionn MacCumhaill.

After about 2km you join a tarred roadway and follow this east and uphill to the entrance for the hotel. Next cross the R664 to the car park opposite and foot the track, signposted 'Rock an Thorabh' ('rock of the bull') for about 1.5km. The Rock, which lies about 40m left of the trail, is a wonderful viewing point for the Golden Vale, Tipperary town and the Slievefelim Hills beyond. Local folklore holds that it was here the runaway lovers, Diarmaid and Gráinne, overnighted as they fled the wrath of cuckolded husband Fionn McCumhail.

Continue along the ridge to reach a point where four tracks intersect. Take the leftmost option and contour the northern slopes of a hill, known

View over the Glen of Aherlow to the Galtee Mountains

locally as the Steeple, for 1km until a minor public road is reached, which you follow uphill to the right for a few hundred metres to reach the unmistakable Jubilee 2000 Memorial. This was constructed as a joint project between the parishes of Tipperary and Bansha/Kilmoyler to celebrate the millennium year. Designed by sculptor Jarlath Daly, the stone depicts the Annunciation, Birth, Crucifixion and Resurrection from the life of Christ and makes an excellent place for a food break.

Once replenished, head off by following the track directly opposite the memorial. As you ascend you will enjoy splendid views across the Glen of Aherlow to the mighty Galtee Mountains with the great necklace of Temple Hill, Lyracappul, Carrignabinnia, Galtymore and Greenane filling the horizon. At the next junction, continue directly ahead on a narrow and sometimes mucky track that ascends and then descends steeply to the four-way junction encountered earlier. This time you take the left option. After approximately 2km you will come to a parking place and viewing point, which is overlooked by a large statue of Christ the King, right hand raised in magisterial blessing to the valley below. This powerfully symbolic figure of Christ, which stands on a plinth of Kilkenny limestone, has now come to signify the glen. It was erected in 1950 when the influence of the Catholic Church in Ireland was at its zenith. Here, it may be worth pausing to note the special attraction of the Glen laid out below you. Unlike many other Irish valleys, this isn't an austere ungiving landscape, but is instead a fertile place that has drawn people to settle here in relative comfort for generations immemorial.

Follow the main road directly ahead for about 100m to the other end of the viewing area where a path leads down wooden steps into the Glen of Aherlow Nature Reserve. This is an admirable local community initiative and consists of over 40 acres of diverse, natural woodland with a well-illustrated nature trail. Follow the arrows through the reserve until a wooden stile leads onto a broad lane as it descends to an attractive stone bridge. You are now standing on an old coach road, which was used by the long cars of Italian immigrant Charles Bianconi who set up Ireland's first system of mass transportation. Beside this is a 'hanging tree', where people were, in the eighteenth century, executed for inconsequential crimes and their bodies left suspended as a warning to passers-by not to tangle with the establishment.

From this bridge descend to another intersection where you go right and then simply foot it the short distance back to your parking place. To survive rural Ireland needs to earn a living, of course, and so you might now say 'thank you' for the parking facilities by popping inside Aherlow House and enjoying a cuppa and a perhaps a bite in the suitably elegant surroundings of the Hunting Lodge Bar.

WALK 27:
The Grange Crag Loop

Grade:	1
Time:	2 hours
Ascent:	160m
Distance:	6 km
Map:	OSi *Discovery* Series sheet 67

Start & Finish: A spider's web of small roads straddles the Tipperary/Kilkenny border, which means that Grange village is not easy to find. To locate the trailhead, go to Urlingford, County Kilkenny and take the R690, signposted Mullinahone. After 2km stay on the R690 as the road divides and continue for almost 5km, passing the entrance to Kilcooley Estate. Beyond this take the first left, following the estate wall, which is reputed to be the longest such in Ireland. After 2km you will enter Grange village. The trailhead is located outside Hogan's Pub.

Suitability: Pleasant and unchallenging walk along dry woodland trails that is best accomplished wearing trainers. The Crag Loop makes for a lovely family outing.

Perhaps you have spent a little too much time in the fast-food lane, and now your priorities are all about pulse-raising self-improvement and rewarding excursions to the outdoors. But while you would appreciate a little more familiarity with the Irish uplands, rambling is your game and you're happy to leave the intensity of highly elevated landscapes to dedicated mountain lovers.

Don't worry, however, for there is a loop walk at the beating heart of rural Tipperary that resolutely circumvents the possibility you will be mugged by gravity. The newly developed

A woodland path on the Crag Loop.

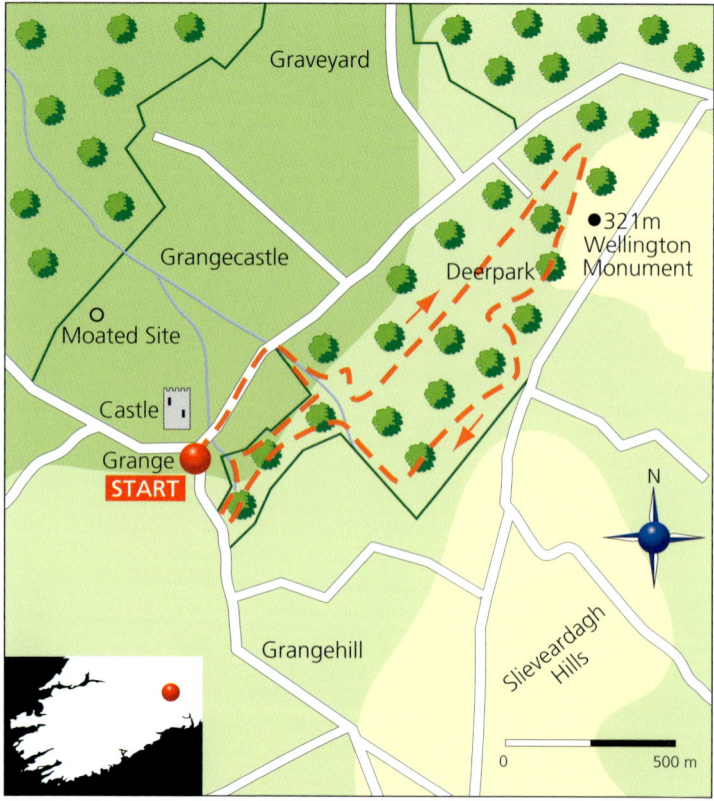

Crag Loop makes for a gentle introduction to green exercising and is an outing calculated to entice even the most committed of couch potatoes into the great outdoors.

Lying close to the Kilkenny border, it explores a most amenable landscape as it saunters through some of the original woodlands that belonged to Kilcooley Abbey and makes an ideal antidote for those suffering 'nature deficit disorder'. This estate, nestling within a green and fertile landscape on the edge of the Slieveardagh Hills, was home to the Ponsonby/Barker family from the 1770s until recently and still holds many compelling resonances from the Ascendancy period of Irish history.

To complete this straightforward circuit, start from outside Hogan's Pub at **S307 564** in the tiny village of Grange, once an out-farm of the abbey and overlooked by a medieval tower house. Follow the purple arrows along the metalled road for 500m to reach the entrance to Grange Crag Woods (right). Take this woodland track to reach an incongruous-looking building on the right that once served as the deep freeze for the Kilcooley

Walk 27: The Grange Crag Loop

The Wellington Monument.

estate. Blocks of ice were cut from frozen ponds or rivers nearby and transported to what was then known as the icehouse, where they were stacked between layers of straw to create a microclimate. Ice, so preserved, could keep throughout the summer and this particular icehouse was used as a cold store for Kilcooley from the eighteenth to mid-twentieth century.

Continue from the icehouse to reach a three-way junction where the arrows are followed right. Ascend along the forest road to reach another three-way junction where you turn a sharp left onto a forestry road that ascends for about a 1km to reach a T-junction where you again go right.

Walk on for about another five minutes until a track on the left takes you uphill to reach a large odd-to-behold construction known locally as the Wellington Monument. It was built in 1817 by William Barker of Kilcooley to commemorate the victory of the Duke of Wellington at the Battle of Waterloo in 1815. Such buildings are generally referred to as follies but usually they served a purpose. Here the idea was clearly to provide a focus to draw people to the highest point of the estate where they would then be impressed by fine views of the great house and wooded glories of the parkland laid out below. Today these views have been further enhanced by the efforts of the local community who have created a viewing point at the top of the edifice, having been funded under the 'adopt a monument' scheme.

Kilcooley Abbey.

Now continue following the arrows along the forest road to a junction with another metalled road where you veer immediately right to re-enter a forest trail. After about 500m the route veers left and crosses open ground where you now enjoy views to the extensive ruins of the twelfth-century Kilcooley Abbey. Built by the Cistercian Order as a sister house of Holycross Abbey on land granted by Donal Mór O'Brien, the last king of Munster, it was dissolved following the English Reformation. Its extensive estates then passed to the Earls of Ormonde, before becoming the property of the Barker family. Unusually for an English family coming to Ireland at this time, they were not granted the lands of Kilcooley but purchased them in 1636 for £4,200. Clearly, however, the Barkers were seen as loyal to the English crown for later they were granted extensive tracks of land in Tipperary and Limerick.

Nearby, but almost obscured among extensive woodlands, the great house at Kilcooley is an impressive Palladian mansion that was first built in the late eighteenth century. The present house dates from 1843 and was constructed after a great fire in 1839 destroyed the original mansion. This conflagration began when a butler of the house, who had been dismissed from his employment by William Ponsonby Barker, set one of the chimneys alight.

Walk 27: The Grange Crag Loop

Woodland near Grange.

Beyond these remarkable edifices, your eye will inevitably be drawn to the Devilsbit Mountain, which provides an austere backdrop to the otherwise serene, pastoral lowlands below.

All too soon the views are obscured when you enter mature broadleaf woodland and swing right to descend by a stream and exit onto a track. Continue (left) following green and purple arrows along the woodland track for almost 1km to almost reach a tarred roadway. Don't go onto the roadway; instead follow the walking arrows sharply right and after a time take the next left which allows you rejoin your outward route. Now return to Grange village, and, as an added treat, why not quench your thirst in the old-world atmosphere of Hogan's tradition pub?

WALK 28:
Devilsbit Mountain

Option 1
Grade: 2
Time: 1½ hours
Ascent: 240m
Distance: 5km

Option 2
Grade: 3
Time: 3 hours
Ascent: 310m
Distance: 9km

Map: OSi *Discovery* Series sheet 59

Start & Finish: From the R501 Templemore–Borrisoleigh road follow the signs right for Barnane from a crossroads. Continue following the signs marked Borrisnafarney that point straight ahead at the next crossroads. When the road reaches its highest point, park at a large gateway on the right.

Suitability: A generally unchallenging outing suitable for those with moderate fitness. The mountaintop is, however, quite exposed so be prepared with spare clothing and raingear. Great care should also be taken ascending and descending the steep cliffs surrounding the Little Rock and also descending from the Long Rock plateau.

What is it with the Irish uplands and the Devil? Among an abundance of demonic high-country appellations are the Devil's Coachroad in the Mourne Mountains, the Devil's Glen in Wicklow, the Devil's Ladder on Carrauntoohil and the Devil's Punchbowl on Mangerton Mountain. And then there is also the proudly individualistic hill standing sentinel above Templemore, County Tipperary. Other such salient Irish peaks that inescapably draw the eye, such as Brandon, Croagh Patrick and Slieve Gullion, have attracted a mixture of superstition and worship for countless centuries. In this regard, Tipperary's Devilsbit Mountain is no exception.

Every north Tipperary schoolchild will have gazed in fascination at the unmistakeable gash in its flat plateau, which is so clearly visible from the

Walk 28: Devilsbit Mountain

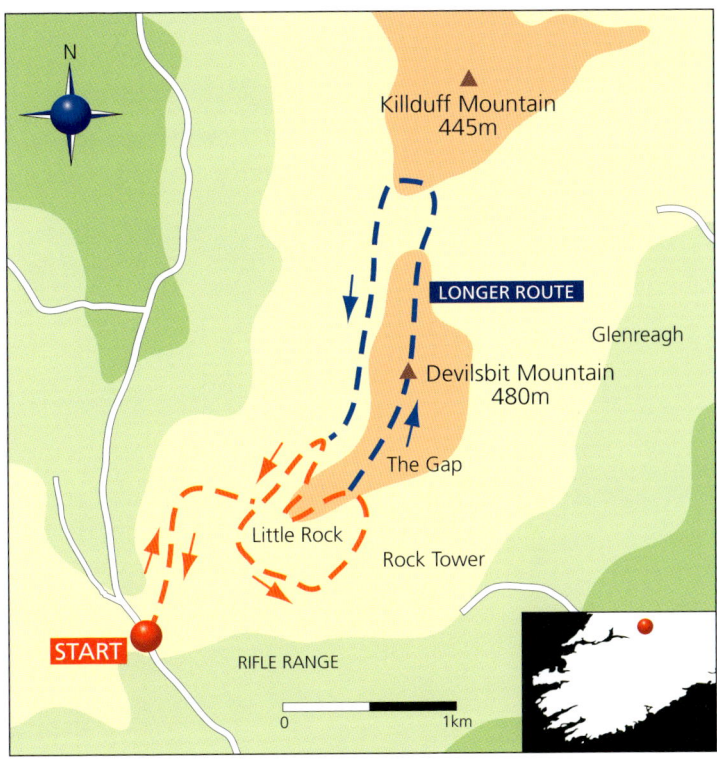

plains below. In explanation they will be told a charming story of a fleeing demon being pursued out of Ireland by St Patrick. Taking an angry bite from its summit plateau, the fiend did a huge service for the Irish tourism industry by dropping it to form the Rock of Cashel.

Unfortunately, scientifically minded spoilsports have been quick to point out that the Devilsbit is composed entirely of sandstone while the Rock of Cashel is a limestone outcrop. Another account holds, however, that the Rock of Cashel was actually formed by the dislodged tooth of the demon. Whatever the veracity of these accounts, we can say with certainty that the mountain offers a charming walk with great views and many other evocative resonances for those who enjoy an easier outing with many historic echoes.

From your parking place, **S043 730**, walk for a leisurely twenty minutes or so, keeping to the left option where the track divides, until an obvious T-junction is reached. Go right and follow around to the south side of the mountain and continue until you notice a prominent round tower on your right. This edifice is not of monastic origin, as you might at first suspect,

Devilsbit from the south

but an eighteenth-century folly built by the wealthy landowning Carden family of Templemore.

The folly was, however, used as the site for a monster meeting in 1832, when, according to local folklore, Ireland's Liberator, Daniel O'Connell, addressed an assembled multitude of 50,000. At the time, he was campaigning against the compulsory payment of tithes (payments of support) to the established Church but, nevertheless, many modern-day historians doubt that he was personally present on the occasion. If he did attend, however, he spoke in English. A fluent Irish speaker, he nevertheless tended to address meetings in English to ensure that the newspapers of the day would print his words. The downside was, of course, that in this way he unwittingly contributed further to the rapid decline of spoken Irish, which took place during the nineteenth century.

At this point, go left and follow the track steeply upwards. To your right you will pass an altar and shrine. On a late July Sunday each year – known locally as Rock Sunday – the shrine here is the scene for the celebration of

Walk 28: Devilsbit Mountain

Mass. This is just one example of the long-standing tradition of pattern-day pilgrimages, which take place annually on many other mountains across Ireland and are, for the most part, examples of the Christianisation of earlier pagan worship.

Continue upwards and you are soon within the actual gap that forms the Devilsbit proper. This turns out to be a rather mundane col, but the sense of history is maintained by the fact that it was in a cave in the nearby cliffs that the priceless Book of Dimma was reputedly discovered. This is a beautifully illuminated eighth-century gospel created at nearby St Cronan's Abbey, Roscrea, which now resides in the National Museum in Dublin. The entrance to the cave was later blocked as a safety precaution with the result that its exact location has been lost in the mists of time.

Now square your shoulders and head left towards the summit of what is known locally as the Little Rock. A short, but steep, scramble past a statue of the Blessed Virgin is required to reach the actual top, which is crowned by a large cross that was built to celebrate the Marian Year of 1954 and is now spectacularly floodlit by night. Here you are rewarded

View south from the Devilsbit.

Sunset at the Devilsbit Gap (Courtesy C.Needham)

with views to Lough Derg and the Slieve Bloom Mountains, while to the south you gaze across the fertile plains of Tipperary bounded in the far distance by the great upland ring consisting of the Galtee, Comeragh and Knockmealdown Mountains.

Descend from the mountaintop by an alternative track on the opposite side from which you approached the summit. This track first skirts a forest on the left and then swings round to enter a wood, before joining a wider track. Go left at this point and continue until you reach the three-way junction encountered earlier. Here turn right to arrive back at your car, having enjoyed an exhilarating but not overly demanding outing.

Option 2

If you prefer a longer outing you can extend your walk by retracing your steps from the Marian Year Cross to the Devilsbit Gap and then following a track that ascends to a plateau known as the Long Rock, which in recent years has become an occasional playground for rock climbers. Continue through heathery terrain to the trig point that represents the summit of Devilsbit Mountain proper (480m) before using a small gully with care to descend steeply from the plateau.

Next follow a rough track with forestry to your left until it joins a green road leading through a gate near a large communications mast. Swing left here and return along a forest roadway that leads you back to the original T–junction from where it is a twenty-minute stroll to your start point. This will allow you the time to reflect, perhaps, that the Devilsbit is a classic example of an 'espresso mountain' – small in stature, but packing a big punch.